Increase Your Score in 3 MINUTES a Day SAT Critical Reading

Also in this series

Increase Your Score in 3 Minutes a Day: SAT Essay,
McCutcheon and Schaffer

Increase Your Score in 3 MINUTES a Day

SAT Critical Reading

Randall McCutcheon and James Schaffer, Ph.D.

McGraw-Hill

New York Chicago San Francisco Lisbon London Madrid Mexico City
Milan New Delhi San Juan Seoul Singapore Sydney Toronto

For my grandmother
—Randall McCutcheon

To Mary Lynn, for her unwavering love and support,
and to Suzanne, Sarah, and Stephen,
who make it all worthwhile.
—James Schaffer

1 2 3 4 5 6 7 8 9 0 LBM/LBM 3 2 1 0 9 8 7 6 5 4

ISBN 0-07-144041-0

Interior design by Cheryl McLean
Interior illustrations:
Pages vii, 22, and 36 © 2003 ZITS Partnership. Reprinted with special permisison of King Features Syndicate.
Pages xii and 62 © Sidney Harris. Reprinted with permission.
Pages 7 and 41 © 2003 Hilary B. Price. Reprinted with special permission of King Features Syndicate.
Page 27 © 1997 ZITS Partnership. Reprinted with special permission of King Features Syndicate.
Page 46 Calvin and Hobbes © 1990 Watterson. Reprinted by permission of Universal Press Syndicate. All rights reserved.
Page 68 © The New Yorker Collection 1996 Tom Cheney from cartoonbank.com. All rights reserved.
Page 86 by David Ernest Lyon

This book is printed on acid-free paper.

Contents

Preface

If you pick up a paper only to glance at the comics, chances are that you—like Jeremy—are more smart aleck than smart. But you are not alone. Researcher William Albert says, "You can walk through whole neighborhoods of houses in this country that do not contain books or magazines—unless you count catalogs."

More and more people who can read, don't. These people who don't read are known as aliterates. In the *Washington Post* article "The No-Book: Skim It and Weep," aliteracy is described as "an invisible liquid, seeping through our culture, nigh on impossible to pinpoint or defend against."

So how pervasive is aliteracy? Kylene Beers, a professor of reading at the University of Houston, says, "About 100 percent of first-graders walk in on the first day and are interested in this thing called reading. Eighty percent of graduating seniors tell us they will never voluntarily pick up a book again."

Big mistake. You need to read as much as possible. It's not about time. It's about choices. Do you check out what's happening at the mall or check out a book? Sim City or *A Tale of Two Cities*? You must decide each time.

Your first good choice today is to read this book. If you follow the advice contained in these pages, you will increase your score on the Critical Reading section of the SAT. But there is a greater purpose here. This book will help you rediscover the joy of reading. And that, dear reader, is no laughing matter.

—Randall J. McCutcheon

Acknowledgments

The authors would like to thank the following:

Jane Durso
David Lyon
David Huston
Stephen Davis
Ben Silberman
Dee Schaffer
Tom Schaffer

Introduction

From the Greek philosophy of a filled storehouse to the statue in the film *Animal House*, we have been reminded that "Knowledge Is Good." Consider this sage advice in Al Franken's book *Oh, the Things I Know!*:

> *It doesn't matter what you learn, just that you remain committed to learning. Make a solemn pledge to learn at least one new thing a week. This week I'm learning the names of the Great Lakes. Next week I'm learning Italian. But that's next week.*

Then again, maybe you don't have time to learn Italian next week. Or much else. This book offers you an efficient way to master Critical Reading skills. *Pronto.*

The first thing you need to understand is that the changes to the SAT haven't greatly affected the Critical Reading questions. "Similar" is the word used by the College Board. Now more of a reading assessment, so says the College Board, this section will include shorter reading passages along with the existing longer passages. Sentence-completion questions remain, but the analogies are gone.

Please note that the following kinds of questions may be asked about the passages:

- **Vocabulary in Context questions.** By studying words in context, you must be able to determine their meanings.
- **Literal Comprehension questions.** Your understanding of specific information directly stated in the passage will be assessed.

- **Extended Reading questions.** These questions are the most challenging. Information must be analyzed and synthesized. You may be asked to evaluate the assumptions of an author. The College Board states that you should know how "to identify cause and effect, make inferences, recognize implications, and follow the logic of an argument."

Simple enough, you say. Unfortunately, more than 600,000 of the freshmen entering college in a recent year enrolled in a remedial reading, writing, or math class. That would be about 29 percent of the entire freshman class. Evidently, being able to read is not a prerequisite for college admission. Education reporter John Cloud asks the obvious question: "Should you be allowed into college if you don't read well enough to understand your local paper?"

Comedian Dave Chappelle might respond: "A jump shot is a terrible thing to waste." Of course, life might not have been a slam dunk for you. Coach may never have sent you into the game. What

"CAN'T YOU GUYS READ?"

then? Casey McCall, a character on the television show "Sports Night," once explained Napoleon's strategy at Waterloo. According to McCall, Napoleon had a two-part plan. The first part: "Just show up." The second part: "See what happens." There is a lesson for you here. If you follow Napoleon's strategy in preparing for the Critical Reading passages, you will likely suffer the same defeat.

This book offers a plan that works. And you won't have to skip to your Waterloo.

Making This Book Work for You

We didn't exaggerate. You can significantly improve your chances for a higher score on the SAT by studying this book for three minutes a day. OK, we exaggerated slightly. Conscientious students (and slow readers) may want to invest a few more minutes each day. Practice and review. Practice and review.

In fact, Dr. Tom Fischgrund, author of *Perfect 1600 Score: The Seven Secrets of Acing the SAT*, argues that you "can't overemphasize the importance of SAT review." His study of students who do well on the SAT concluded that your score depends more on preparation than on brains or pure luck.

If that sounds a little too time-consuming for you, remember what celebrity Jennifer Lopez said when asked what she got on the SAT. J.Lo replied, "Nail polish." Apocryphal story or not, just think of what J.Lo might have accomplished if only she had studied. To paraphrase Lewis Carroll, they are called lessons because they lessen from day to day.

The "lessens" are explained below. Pay attention. A good manicurist is hard to find. And costly.

The Basic Approach

The Eight-Week, 3-Minute-a-Day Plan

Day 1: Study the "Introduction" and "Making This Book Work for You" sections.

Days 2–21: Study one Principle each day. Then, three times throughout the day, review in your head the essential ideas taught in that day's principle. The next morning in the shower say aloud those same essential ideas. Repeat. And not just the shampoo. Lather, too.

Days 22–31: Begin mastering the Strategies. Use the same daily routine that you learned with the Principles. One Strategy each day.

Days 32–46: Read and answer the question(s) for one Practice Passage a day. Review the Principles and Strategies that apply to the question(s).

Days 47–56: Review the Strategies one more time.

Day 57: Celebrate. Take as long as you like.

The Last-Minute Approach ... or SAT-CPR

You've procrastinated. The SAT is only a week away. How do you resuscitate your chances for Critical Reading success? Our prescription: choose one of the following two protocols.

Protocol 1: Skip the Principles sections. For three days, spend the minutes you've allocated for study to the Strategies. Do five of the passages each day over the next three days. On the seventh day, rest and review.

Protocol 2: This protocol requires additional time each day but is a more thorough "treatment." Thus, the prognosis for recovery is better. On the first two days, study the Principles section. Work on the Practice Passages for the next two days. On the seventh day, rest and review.

What is that word that a doctor shouts when an emergency-room patient goes into cardiac arrest? Oh yeah, "Clear."

CLEAR!

Good news. You have a pulse. So defibril . . . later. Study now.

PRINCIPLES OF READING

There is something in the American character that is secretly hostile to the act of aimless reading.
—Anna Quindlen

America values sociability and community, notes novelist and former *New York Times* columnist Anna Quindlen, and unfortunately too often associates "nose in the book" readers with loners and losers. But learning to read well is as vital to your success as it has been to Quindlen's, in college and beyond.

In the following pages you will find fifteen reading principles that are tried-and-true techniques. They will help you increase your reading speed, know what to read and what to skip, learn how to mark up a passage to make review easy, quickly identify the thesis and supporting points, summarize what you've read to help find answers, discover what words mean from their contexts, and much more.

The only losers in the SAT game are those who can't read. So buckle up your courage and prepare to become a topflight reader.

Rev That Engine, Parnelli!

Good readers have the mind-set of a race-car driver. They press the pedal to the metal on the straightaways and slow down on the curves. In other words, they vary their reading speed depending on what they want to accomplish. You should too.

The long passages in the SAT Critical Reading test range from 400 to 850 words. Your aim should be to spend no more than about three to four minutes reading each passage. To do so, you should try to average at least 200 words per minute. That will leave you about forty seconds to answer each question.

The average college student reads between 250 and 350 words per minute on fiction and nontechnical material. Some people can read a thousand words per minute or even faster, but the SAT isn't about speed-reading—it's about reading for meaning.

Nevertheless, research has shown that the faster you read, the more likely you are to remember what you've read. Slow reading—plodding along word by word—inhibits understanding. With a little guided practice, most people can double their reading speed without lowering their comprehension.

Here are some techniques that may help you increase how fast you read:

1. **Avoid regressing** (going back over what you've already read). Rereading words and phrases is a habit that will slow your reading down to a snail's pace. Usually, it is unnecessary to reread words, as the ideas you want are explained and elaborated more fully later in the passage.

If you read slowly, your mind has time to wander. Even worse, if you find yourself doing so, this reflects both an inability to concentrate and a lack of confidence in your comprehension skills (think of the student who never hears the directions the first time).

2. **Develop a wider eye span.** This will help you read more than one word at a glance. Since written material is less meaningful if read word by word, this will help you learn to read by phrases or thought units.

3. **Learn to adjust your rate to your purpose in reading and to the difficulty of the material.** The effective reader adjusts his or her rate; the ineffective reader uses the same rate for all types of material.

   Suppose you took a 100-mile mountain trip by car. You might plan to average about fifty miles an hour, but in reality, you slow down to twenty on some hills and curves and speed up to seventy on certain straightaways. The same concept holds true with reading.

   In general, slow down when you find the following:

   - unfamiliar terms not immediately clear from context
   - difficult sentence or paragraph structure
   - abstract concepts
   - detailed technical material (complicated directions, for example)

   On the other hand, increase your reading speed when you encounter:

   - simple material with few ideas that are new to you
   - unnecessary examples or illustrations
   - broad, general ideas or ideas that are restatements of previous ones

Keep your reading attack flexible; adjust your rate from passage to passage and within each passage. The crucial skill is to be able to change speed, to know when to slow down or speed up.

Pacing is particularly important on Critical Reading—if you spend too much time reading the passages, you won't leave enough time for the questions. Don't sweat the details. Don't waste time reading and rereading parts you don't understand. Make sure you leave time for answering the questions, which is what really counts.

Know When and What to Skip

What you bring to your reading is far more important than the words themselves. All the knowledge you've gained from life so far—both the knowledge of the world and the knowledge of how written works are constructed—helps you know what a passage means. In a strange sense, you know what you're going to read before you even start.

Let's take a closer look at that apparent paradox. The secret of reading efficiently is to sample the text and make predictions. The reader takes chances and risks making errors, in order to predict what a passage means. Unless the reader feels free to take chances and make mistakes, he or she can never make any real headway.

We read to identify meaning, not to identify letters or words. A reader cannot process letters, words, and meanings all at the same time. Natural limitations in our memory systems prevent it (for example, we can remember phone numbers, but just barely—seven digits is about our max). We slow down to look at letters, letter clusters, or words only when we are surprised or confused—when what we expected to read wasn't there.

The reader guesses the meaning of unfamiliar words from context or else just skips them. Even in textbook or technical material, the best strategy is to skip a new word the first time it appears, expecting it to be explained or defined contextually before too long. Of course, if the new word is not explained, keeps reappearing, and seems to be important, then the reader can use a dictionary or guess. But consider if you are engrossed in a personal letter from a friend or an exciting novel. Do you stop when you read an unfamiliar word? Of course not.

As a good reader, you take an active role, bringing to bear your knowledge of the world and of the particular topic in the passage. You read as though you expect the passage to make sense. Therefore, with difficult or unfamiliar material, the best approach may be to push ahead, especially on the first reading, trusting that the reading will become easier as you continue predicting meaning, making guesses, and taking chances.

If you didn't do these things, psycholinguists tell us, you couldn't read at all. Their research suggests that the reader relies as little as possible on visual information. Good readers sample the passage economically, searching for major points and key terms.

What happens when your predictions go awry (as they will, from time to time)? You correct surprises by circling back when tentative interpretations or predictions are not successful. At the same time, however, you maintain enough speed to overcome the limitations of the visual processing and memory systems.

Crystal Ball Grazing

Look deeply into this crystal ball. Can you see your future? Yes, the one where your house is featured on MTV's "Cribs" and you've just been signed to a multimillion-dollar contract to promote a new soft drink.

Predicting the future isn't just for soothsayers and television prophets. Readers, too, proceed by making predictions about the passage. We are rarely aware that we are making predictions for the simple reason that our predictions are usually so good. Our predictions rarely let us down, even when we read a book for the first time.

What exactly do we predict when we read? The fundamental answer is meaning. Prediction is the reason that the brain is not overwhelmed by all the possible alternatives in a passage; for example, if you reach the bottom of a page and see this sentence: "The captain told the crew to drop an-", you don't really need to turn the page to know that an "anchor" is just about to plop into the sea. We expect what the writer is likely to say because consciously or not, we are continually making predictions about the text.

Let's look at how this might work in the SAT Critical Reading exam. Suppose you find a passage that begins like this:

> *One evening in late January, Peter Dut, twenty-one, leads his two teenage brothers through the brightly lit corridors of the Minneapolis airport, trying to mask his confusion.*

We immediately grasp the basic situation: we have a narrative involving several characters (Peter and his two brothers), a setting (January in Minneapolis, brrrr!), and a conflict (Peter is confused).

What we're not told—why Peter is in Minneapolis in the first place and why he's so confused—helps stimulate our desire to predict. We expect to find answers to those questions as the passage continues, and by predicting what those answers will be we become more active readers. Here's the next sentence:

> *Two days earlier, the brothers, refugees from Africa, encountered their first light switch and their first set of stairs.*

Part of the mystery is solved. We know the boys are from Africa, and from a very undeveloped part, apparently. But part of the mystery remains open: how is it that they have come to Minneapolis? This process will be repeated over and over again as we read. We will find a few answers that in turn lead to more questions.

Let's see what happens next:

> *An aid worker in Nairobi demonstrated the flush toilet to them—also the seat belt, the shoelace, the fork. And now they find themselves alone in Minneapolis, three bone-thin African boys confronted by a swirling river of white faces and rolling suitcases.*

Images from Africa (the "river of white faces") blend in the boys' imaginations with new sensations ("rolling suitcases") to create a cultural jumble. Now we can predict what the narrative is heading toward: a series of cultural encounters between these African boys and American technology. And indeed, as we read in the article "The Lost Boys" by Sara Corbett, we learn the story of some 3,600 Sudanese refugees who have come to the United States to find new lives.

As you read the SAT passages, keep asking yourself: Where is this headed? What can I expect to find? Making guesses and predictions will keep you alert and engaged as a reader. It puts you in control.

Pay special attention to first and last words of a paragraph—do they remind you of something you read in the previous paragraph or help prepare you for the succeeding one? Look for parallels in content and style. Often writers will emphasize a point by repeating the structure of a particular sentence or repeating a particularly significant word.

Finally, polish up that mental crystal ball you've been saving for just this occasion.

Writing Between the Lines

You ought to hold something in your hand while you read. No, not a glass of iced tea. Not even a Snickers, though that's not a bad idea. What we're talking about is a pencil.

The pencil represents your alertness. It acts as a symbol of the active reader. Use the pencil as you read to mark the passage.

Students are sometimes reluctant to write on a book. If the book belongs to the school, that's a good policy. But if the book belongs to you, make it your own and mark all over it. That's the real way to claim it as your property.

In the case of the SAT test, you're free to mark up the reading passages. Don't miss this opportunity. Marking the passage accomplishes two very important goals:

1. It keeps you alert. With that pencil in hand, you have the sense that you're doing something as you read, not simply absorbing information passively.
2. It makes it easy to review. When you go back over a passage, you can quickly return to key points and terms that you've already identified.

Here are a couple of techniques to help you mark a passage effectively and efficiently:

- Underline key points or ideas.
- Use vertical lines in the margins when the section you want to highlight is too long to underline.

- Use stars or asterisks to indicate the thesis statement of a passage.
- Use numbers to indicate key supporting details.
- Circle key words or terms. These can be terms that seem especially important or, occasionally, terms that seem to be used in a strange or unusual way.
- Write in the margins or at the top or bottom of the page. These are the places to jot down a few thoughts. Make note of any questions you might have. In the case of the SAT, if you have looked ahead at the questions, write down possible answers—before you look at the answers the test makers offer.

Keeping a pencil handy as you read makes reading a more active, physical process. If you can do something to keep your body (as well as your mind) in motion, you have a much better chance of understanding and remembering what you read (see Strategy 5 for additional ideas).

X-Ray Vision

Remember the Terminator? In those movies, the main character is a robot that looks human. In other words, beneath his flesh and blood lies a metal skeleton (never mind that the actor who played him, Arnold Schwarzenegger, was better at playing robots than humans).

An x-ray would have quickly revealed the Terminator's identity. Using x-ray vision (metaphorically speaking), you can also quickly discover the skeleton, or structure, beneath the surface of the words in a passage. The surface features, whether of text or robot, can be deceiving, but if you can discern what lies beneath, you will have a true sense of the passage's meaning.

You can learn to use x-ray vision to help you answer three questions about any given chunk of prose:

1. **What is the passage about?** By quickly scanning the entire passage, you can grasp a sense of the writer's topic and probably something about the writer's approach.

   Is the work mainly fact or fiction? Is the work from the world of science (you'll be tipped off, most likely, by the presence of technical terms and references to experiments) or social sciences (trends, correlations, causes, and consequences)? Is the text written in first person or third person? The answers to these questions help set the stage for this one:

2. **What are the parts or sections of the passage?** If the writer is worth her salt, she will have presented some support for her main point. Can you recognize the nature of that support? Typically, an author will present several reasons or examples

to convince the reader that the thesis is true. If you can recognize these subpoints, you will be able to see the passage fall neatly into sections.

Most passages can be organized into a hierarchy with the thesis on top, supporting points below, and explanatory details even farther down. Once you see the pattern, you can zero in on what you really want to know or what question you're trying to answer. Finally, use your x-ray vision to answer this last question:

3. **How do the parts fit together?** Each passage may have a beginning, middle, and end, but not necessarily in that order. So pay attention to transition words and terms. Some transition words tell you that the writer is continuing a particular chain of thought by adding information. These words and phrases include: *additionally, also, moreover, not only, but, another, furthermore, moreover,* and *for example*. Other transition words and phrases may signal a change or reversal: *however, on the other hand, but,* and *yet*. Still others tell you the writer is reaching a conclusion: *therefore, then, thus, in sum,* and *in short.*

If you have a clear idea of the overall development of the passage, you will be able to answer thesis questions more easily and understand how the various parts of the argument fit together. Be on the lookout for contrasting points of view. Most selections will present one argument and briefly describe a competing or conflicting idea. Fictional passages may pit what the main character thinks against what others think.

It may also be true that your x-ray vision will spot a broken bone, in other words, a flaw, in the passage. Perhaps one of the subpoints is not fully developed, or maybe the thesis comes after some of the supporting information. In any event, learning to develop x-ray vision will reveal to you whatever lurks beneath the surface.

Something Worth Arguing About

The typical SAT reading passage will contain a thesis statement, usually in the first paragraph. The thesis statement will let the reader know, as soon as possible, what argument the passage will make. Identifying this thesis statement is the most important reading task you have.

A thesis is the largest, broadest statement in the passage. It should have these three characteristics:

1. It is something worth arguing about. There is no point in basing a passage on a thesis that is obvious to everyone or that isn't concerned with a significant issue. Read the statement you identify as the thesis, and ask yourself, "So what?" If you can't answer that question, you probably haven't found the true thesis.
2. It is precise. It is not something anyone has trouble understanding and is not so general that it fails to represent a strong position.
3. It is supported by the rest of the passage; it isn't just a springboard that allows the writer to jump into topics having little to do with the thesis.

Let's try that test on the following passage, taken from a *Smithsonian* article by Andrew Curry on the first human flight, that of the Wright brothers at Kitty Hawk in 1903:

As an Air Force test pilot, Lt. Col. Dawn Dunlop has flown dozens of different airplanes, from the nimble F-I SE Strike Eagle fighter to the massive C-17 transport jet to the Russian MIG-21. Stationed at Edwards Air Force Base, she's part of the elite squadron that is putting the cutting-edge F/A-22 Raptor, a jet fighter, through its paces. But the aircraft that Dunlop has had the toughest time controlling was a replica of the Wright brothers' glider. More than once she crash-landed the muslin-skinned craft on to the windswept sands of Kitty Hawk, North Carolina. "It was a real eye-opener," Dunlop recalls of the (bruising) experience last year, part of a commemorative Air Force program. "They've made it so simple to fly today we've forgotten how difficult it was back then."

In this passage, the writer introduces us to an Air Force test pilot, someone who has flown the world's most advanced and sophisticated aircraft. And yet, it turns out, the toughest plane she ever flew was a replica of the Wright brothers' glider. That background, which provides a useful context for the reader, prepares us for the thesis statement—the last sentence in the paragraph. We could paraphrase it like this: "Flying seems simple today, so simple we have forgotten how difficult it was in the beginning of human flight." Does that sentence meet our test?

1. **Is it worth arguing about?** Certainly. The magazine's blurb reinforces the thesis this way: "From the Wright brothers' breakthrough 100 years ago to the latest robot jets, the past century has been shaped by the men and women who got us off the ground." Reviewing the story of the Wright brothers will help us put modern aviation progress in perspective.

2. **Is it precise?** "Back then" in the thesis refers specifically to the Wright brothers and their famous flight in December 1903.

3. **Is it supported by the passage?** Some of the references in the passage to modern aircraft seem at first glance to be off target. But on further reflection, it's clear that they provide a useful contrast to the simplicity of that first flight.

Here's one final test: a good thesis answers a question. What that question is, however, is something you'll have to figure out. In this case, the question might be: why is the Wright brothers' flight significant today? If the thesis statement you've identified in an SAT passage can be viewed as an answer to a question the writer wanted to ask, you have probably zeroed in on just the right sentence.

Summarily Dismissed

Every passage you read will present a different challenge, but being able to summarize what you read will help you become a more active reader, someone who can quickly grasp what he's reading. As you'll discover, being able to say in a few words what has taken someone else a great many can be difficult. But like any other skill, the ability to summarize improves with practice.

Here are a few pointers to get you started. Be prepared, however, to vary your technique to fit the situation.

1. **As you read, pay close attention to the author's purpose.** This will help you distinguish between more important and less important information.

2. **Write a one-sentence summary of the entire passage.** Consider what a newspaper reporter would want to know: the who, what, why, where, when, and how. The idea of a summary is to clarify and condense. Your goal is to create a miniature version of the passage, to repeat its essence but telescoped in size and scale. Summarize the author's ideas in the order in which he has presented them, but avoid following his wording too closely.

3. **Check your summary against the original passage.** Make whatever adjustments are necessary for accuracy and completeness. Notice what you've left out. Is it essential or can it be safely disregarded?

For practice, take a look at the following passage from Jon Krakauer's thrilling book about mountain climbing, *Into Thin Air*:

> *People who don't climb mountains—the great majority of humankind, that is to say—tend to assume that the sport is a reckless, Dionysian pursuit of ever escalating thrills. But the notion that climbers are merely adrenaline junkies chasing a righteous fix is a fallacy, at least in the case of Everest. What I was doing up there had almost nothing in common with bungee jumping or skydiving or riding a motorcycle at 120 miles per hour.*
>
> *Above the comforts of Base Camp, the expedition in fact became an almost Calvinistic undertaking. The ratio of misery to pleasure was greater by an order of magnitude than any other mountain I'd been on; I quickly came to understand that climbing Everest was primarily about enduring pain. And in subjecting ourselves to week after week of toil, tedium, and suffering, it struck me that most of us were probably seeking, above all else, something like a state of grace.*

The most important thing the author tries to do in this passage is to correct a common assumption, namely that mountain climbers do it for thrills. Instead, he argues, climbers endure the work, boredom, and suffering that a climb entails to achieve a state of mind, or a serenity of soul, if you will. A summary statement to that effect might look like this:

> *Contrary to popular opinion, people who climb extreme peaks are seeking food for the soul, not thrills for the gut.*

When you are summarizing, review any sentences you have underlined or highlighted to be sure you haven't left anything out. The main difficulty is to determine what is important and what is not. Some parts of the passage—the introduction, examples, and anecdotes—can probably be ignored. Others, including the author's purpose, theme, and key words, must not be.

Be Chalant

It had been a rough day, so when I walked into the party I was very chalant, despite my efforts to appear gruntled and consolate. I was furling my wieldy umbrella for the coat check when I saw her standing alone in a corner. She was a descript person, a woman in a state of total array. Her hair was kempt, her clothing sheveled, and she moved in a gainly way.

—Jack Winter

Notice anything missing in that passage? How about a few crucial prefixes—those little syllables that appear at the beginnings of words and provide important ingredients of meaning. (For the record, substitute these words in the passage above and see if things make more sense: *nonchalant*, *disgruntled*, *disconsolate*, *unfurling*, *unwieldy*, *nondescript*, *disarray*, *unkempt*, *disheveled*, and *ungainly*.)

Words are not merely groups of letters aimlessly thrown together. They are composed of meaningful elements so arranged as to give each its own significance. For example, many words can be divided into beginnings, middles, and ends. The beginning is a prefix, the middle is the root, and the ending is the suffix.

One of the most economical ways of expanding your vocabulary is to become familiar with the most common affixes (prefixes and suffixes). In doing so, you will acquire clues to the meanings of thousands of words. Furthermore, you will find that spelling becomes easier, for you will see words in their meaningful parts rather than as mere jumbles of letters.

For example, the following English prefixes should already be quite familiar:

after- (later than) as in *afternoon*, *afterward*, and *afterthought*
fore- (before) as in *forehead*, *foreword*, and *forecast*
mis- (bad or wrong) as in *misbehavior*, *misfortune*, and *misfit*

Prefixes often give a negative spin to words. Notice how a prefix turns *stable* into *unstable*, *mature* into *immature*, *adequate* into *inadequate*, and *social* into *antisocial*. Some prefixes, on the other hand, suggest relationships: con- (meaning together) gives us *convoy*, *contain*, and *consent*; circum- (meaning around) yields *circumference*, *circumspect*, and *circumvent*; inter- (meaning between) provides *intercept*, *international*, and *interrupt*.

Suffixes (a word's ending syllable or syllables) also play an important part in determining a word's meaning. Notice what a difference the following suffixes make:

employer versus *employee*
thoughtful versus *thoughtless*
waiter versus *waitress*
changeable versus *changeless*

Sometimes you can even combine a prefix and a suffix to make a word. The ending *-cide* (act of killing), for example, can be combined with a variety of prefixes to give us *homicide*, *suicide*, and *genocide*.

Certainly you can't expect to master every prefix and suffix (though a little practice may pay big dividends). You can use your knowledge of the architecture of words, however—what constitutes their beginning, middle, and end—to make some informed guesses about words you don't know.

Suppose you come across the word *superfluous*. You may be stumped at first, but then you recognize *super-* as a prefix. You know the words *superman* and *superhuman*, so you make a guess that *super* means "over" or "above." Now for the final part of the word: "Hmm, *fluous* sort of looks like *fluid*, so perhaps *superfluous* means 'extra fluid.'" That's not far, by the way, from the dictionary definition—"overflow."

So when you're faced with a difficult word in the SAT exam, divide and conquer. Break the word into its various parts, and see if you can transform several small meanings into one large one.

The Power of Pivot

Imagine a basketball game. The Harlem Globetrotters throw the ball to their center, Meadowlark Lemon. Lemon twists and turns; he takes a step this way, he takes a step that way, but he never moves one foot (his pivot foot)—until he's sure which way he's going. Pivot, the act of turning or changing direction, is a key point in basketball and in writing.

An [illegible] reader will be on the lookout for pivot words and phrases such as *however*, *but*, and *on the other hand*. These words, also called hinge or elbow words, mark a quick turn in the direction the passage is taking from positive to negative, perhaps, or from one point to another.

Let's look at an example. Here is a passage from Joshua P. Warren's book *How to Hunt Ghosts*:

> *Humans have been experiencing things they cannot explain for thousands of years. Most of the world's religions are based on the concept of a spiritual world, or an invisible dimension of existence that transcends our own. However, despite the centuries of "ghostly encounters," such episodes are still considered unexplained.*

Note that pivot word, *however*. Everything in the passage before *however* suggests that humans have long believed in the presence of the supernatural. Everything after *however*, however, suggests that most people don't give any credence to these beliefs. The writer warns the reader with *however* that "that was then, this is now."

Pivot words can sometimes mark a major shift in time, place, or orientation. In this passage from Bill Vaughn's story "Skating Home

Backward," the narrator talks about a childhood dream to ice-skate up the stream beside his house:

> *In the winter, the creek became a different sort of sanctuary. It was a snap to skate the 300 yards from our place to the lagoon where the Missouri accepted the stream, but what I yearned to do was skate to the creek's headwaters, where I would live in tree houses and steal chickens from ranches. It wasn't just the easy pleasure of forward motion that seduced me when I took to the ice, but also the chance to escape all the unpredictable emotional weather back at the house. Yet I never got farther upstream than three miles. When I was old enough to mount a serious quest, it was too late. The creek began running the color of old blood, poisoned by acids and heavy metals leached from the coal mines. The frogs and the fish disappeared first, and finally the turtles. And then it dried up.*

This passage has a small pivot word and another more significant one. The small one is *but*. It highlights the difference between easy tasks (skating 300 yards from home to a nearby lagoon) and difficult ones (skating to the creek's headwaters). The large elbow word is *yet*, not a very impressive looking word, but one that turns the whole passage on its head. Everything before *yet* is youthful, hopeful, and optimistic—about quests and dreams.

What comes after *yet*, however, is dismal—serious adult reality. The creek becomes poisoned by toxic runoff, the frogs and fish die off, and eventually the creek itself disappears. That's a lot of work for a little word like *yet*, and yet, this pivot word is up to the challenge.

Wordlubbers, Beware

As I was going to St. Ives
I met a man with seven wives.
Every wife had seven sacks.
Every sack had seven cats.
Every cat had seven kits.
Kits, cats, sacks, and wives:
How many were going to St. Ives?

If your answer to this riddle is 2,402 (seven times seven times seven times seven plus one), slap yourself silly. You fell for some misdirection. The correct answer, of course, is one—the narrator, or "I," in the poem—who is headed toward St. Ives. All the others he meets must be going in the opposite direction.

This little riddle is a telling example of how nearly all of us can be fooled from time to time by words. By becoming more aware of a few simple language traps, however, you can make yourself much less likely to stumble on the SAT.

Here, for example, is a question that appears to test grammar: Which is correct: "Nine and seven is fifteen" or "Nine and seven are fifteen?" If you said "are," nice going; that's the better of the two answers. But neither answer is correct. Nine and seven are sixteen. (Yes, you're right, we're not supposed to be talking about the math portion of the test right now.) The lesson here is that we often look for the wrong thing because we misunderstood the question. Read difficult questions twice to be sure you know what kind of answer is being sought.

Sometimes we are victims of our own assumptions. Can you solve this puzzle:

> *A doctor is about to operate on a little boy. "This boy is my son," exclaims the doctor. The doctor is correct, yet the doctor isn't the boy's father. What's going on?*

This puzzle seems to stump just about everyone, though the answer is really quite simple. The doctor is the boy's mother. Our assumption about doctors—that they're mostly male—is unconscious, but it acts like blinders, keeping us from looking around to find alternative explanations. Be wary of personal prejudices and opinions that may distract you from the real import of a passage.

Here, a different kind of assumption can get in the way:

> *Two men play five games of checkers, and each wins the same number of games. There are no ties. How can this be?*

If you're stumped, you're in good company. From the way the statement reads, it's easy to assume that the two men have been playing each other. But, in fact, they haven't. The only way they could each win the same number of games is if they were competing against other players. Don't read more into the answer; take it at face value.

Effective reading always requires you to use what you know. Learn to apply the knowledge you've acquired in ten years of school (and more of life). For example, can you figure out this answer:

> *A rope ladder hangs over the side of a ship. The ladder is twelve feet long, and the rungs are one foot apart, with the lowest rung resting on the surface of the ocean. The tide is rising at six inches an hour. How long will it take before the first three rungs of the ladder are underwater?*

Landlubbers beware. If you said four hours, you must be from the Midwest. As the tide rises, of course, so do boats. The rung resting on the surface of the ocean will still be there no matter how high or how low the tide might be. As the old saying goes, "A rising tide lifts all boats."

And don't let your boat sink in the SAT exam because of overreading, overinterpreting, unwarranted assumptions, or failure to apply some common sense.

Get a Clue, Holmes

Suppose a stranger were to meet several of your friends before he met you. Would he form an impression of the kind of person you are from the people you spend time with? Probably. Most of us have much in common with the company we keep.

This idea may help you understand how it is possible to learn the meaning of a word without ever looking it up in a dictionary. Good readers, in fact, do this all the time. We say they learn the meaning of a word through its context.

Researchers have shown that most readers could skip every fifth word and still have a good understanding of what they read. Try this sentence from a newspaper, for example:

> *Some working parents wistfully ________ considered keeping their toddlers ________ from day care in ________ hope of isolating them ________ runny noses, coughs, and ________.*

If your guesses were (in order) *have*, *home*, *the*, *from*, and *germs*, you win the blue ribbon. Even if you only guessed one or two correct answers, you still deduced the words from context.

What this example suggests is that we use the words we recognize in a sentence to help us predict what the other words will be and what they will mean. Pay special attention, for example, to the nonitalicized words in this passage from John McPhee's book on Alaska, *Coming into the Country*:

> *Anchorage has a thin history. Something of a* precursor *of the modern pipeline camps, it began in 1914 as a collection of*

> *tents pitched to shelter workers building the Alaska Railroad. For decades, it was a wooden-sidewalked, gravel-streeted town. Then, remarkably early, as cities go, it developed an urban slum, and both homes and commerce began to abandon its core. The* exodus *was so rapid that the central business district never wholly* consolidated, *and downtown Anchorage is even more miscellaneous than outlying parts of the city.*

Let's see how other words in the passage can help us discover the meaning of *precursor*, *exodus*, and *consolidated*. (Pretend for a moment that those words are unfamiliar.)

The first three sentences of the passage contain many references to time—*history*, *began*, *1914*, *for decades*. This helps us recognize that *precursor* has something to do with time. The prefix, *pre*, is another clue. This prefix should suggest "before" to you (think of *preview*, *predict*, and *precaution*). Thus, *precursor* must be something that comes before in time; try to think of a synonym—in this case, *predecessor*.

Exodus might be a bit tougher. You know you've heard it before; perhaps you even know it as the name of the second book of the Old Testament. But what the heck does it mean? In the context of this passage, we know that whatever it is, it happens rapidly. It also appears to have something to do with abandon—in the previous sentence we learned that home and business owners have left the city core. The beginning of the word, *ex-*, seems to be a hint (you think of *exit* and *ex-girlfriend*, so it means out or on the outs). Pending further information, which may come later in the passage, you decide *exodus* must mean a hasty departure.

The big clue for the final word, *consolidated*, comes in the form of an antonym or its opposite, in other words. The author of the passage draws a contrast between *consolidated* and *miscellaneous*. Because the city core never consolidated, we are told, it remains miscellaneous. So if we can figure out what *miscellaneous* means, we can be reasonably sure that *consolidated* is just the opposite.

Luckily, you remember that your father had a manila folder labeled "Miscellaneous" lying on the kitchen table the last time he was working on his taxes. He said he threw everything that didn't fit anyplace else in there. If *miscellaneous* means an unorganized mish-mash of things, then *consolidated* must mean to unite or combine into a coherent whole. Bingo, you've scored 100 percent on this vocabulary test.

Coming to Terms

Not all words are equal. Or perhaps more accurately, not all words have the same value in a given passage. Inevitably, a writer uses certain words in an especially significant way—either because these words are crucial to the point he or she wants to make or because the author is using a familiar word in a new way. In either case, the writer is turning some words into terms—terms the reader would do well to heed.

We can put it more bluntly: you must spot the important words in a passage and figure out how the author is using them. This challenge has two steps: First, you have to find the important words, the words that make a difference. Second, you have to determine what these words mean as precisely as possible.

So, you ask, how can we tell which of the hundreds of words in a passage are the most important? One way is to notice words that give you trouble. If you notice a word that you don't understand or any word that seems to be used in a peculiar way, you may have located some of the words an author is treating with special significance.

An author may also place explicit stress on certain words. She may, for example, use quotation marks or italics to mark an important word. Notice in the following passage by Dava Sobel how one word appears in italics:

> As a child, I learned the trick for remembering the difference between latitude and longitude. The latitude lines, the *parallels*, really do stay parallel to each other as they girdle the globe from the Equator to the poles in a series of shrinking concentric rings. The meridians of

> longitude go the other way: They loop from the North Pole to the South and back again in great circles of the same size, so they all converge at the ends of the Earth.

Sobel wants to call the reader's attention to the literal meaning of *parallels* as a memory device. Because the reader will read the words *latitude* and *longitude* over and over again throughout this book, the author wants to make a clear and memorable distinction between the two.

Other special words may not be quite as easy to find. Every field of knowledge has its own special vocabulary. In the Sobel passage above, we find these words and phrases: *lines*, *poles*, *concentric rings*, *meridians*, and *converge*—all key terms for mapmakers. Use your general knowledge to help you. You will certainly recognize some scientific terms in an article about, say, microorganisms, and the words you don't recognize are probably scientific terms. You don't necessarily need to know these terms. It may be enough that you can recognize them for what they are.

A third way to identify a key term is to notice when the author makes a fuss. Again in the Sobel passage, she makes a point of defining meridians for the reader ("They loop from the North Pole to the South and back again in great circles of the same size"). Here the writer has anticipated the reader's confusion or, perhaps, lack of knowledge and dealt with the situation head-on.

In short, the relatively small set of words that express an author's main ideas make up his special vocabulary. They are the words that carry his argument. That means these words should be important for you, too, as a reader. Typically, a number of SAT questions will ask you about a key term in the passage. We don't want to miss the forest for the trees, but sometimes it pays to give special attention to a few key words.

Some things are ha…
unusually difficult pass…
Regroup.

What makes some Critical Reading passages difficult? You may be given a passage with a particularly obscure topic. The passage may contain abstract ideas or unfamiliar terms. Or you may be intimidated by the subject matter (quantum mechanics, for example, or nuclear fusion). In any of those cases, consider these tactics:

1. **What does the author discuss most?** In this passage from "The Perfect Fire," Sean Flynn describes in colorful detail the various implements a firefighter might carry:

> *Every firefighter carries a tool. Some have hoses and ropes, but everyone else wields a piece of medieval hardware—a flat-head ax, for instance, or a Boston Rake, which looks like an old vaudeville hook, except it's made of solid iron and can rip out a plaster ceiling in three swift strokes. Some prefer a Haligan, a rod of hardened steel roughly the size of a baseball bat, with one end flattened into a two-pronged claw. The other end, a flat wedge that can slip between a door and a jamb to pry it open, is attached perpendicularly to the shaft. Next to that, also at a 90-degree angle to the shaft, is an adze, a pear-sized steel point that can puncture the most solid walls and doors.*

The odd names of these tools—Boston Rake, Haligan, and adze—may put you off for a moment. "How am I supposed to know what these things are?" you might ask. But don't be discouraged. The author has given us plenty of clues.

For starters, the whole passage is about tools (see sentence #1). You're familiar with tools—they have a design and a function. If you don't completely understand one, you might understand the other. So, for example, the Boston Rake is hard to picture, but it rips out plaster ceilings. What the Haligan does is not entirely clear, but it looks like a baseball bat. By noticing the stress the author places on tools, you can gloss over the details—firefighters have weapons. You don't need much more at this point.

2. **Don't get thrown by the fancy language—just push past it.** Try the following passage. It concerns two of the most important endocrine glands (you know, the ones that regulate our hormones):

> *The hypothalamus regulates the internal environment through the autonomic system. For example, it helps control heartbeat, body temperature, and water balance. The hypothalamus also controls the glandular secretions of the pituitary gland. The pituitary, a small gland about 1 cm in diameter, is connected to the hypothalamus by a stalklike structure. The pituitary has two portions: the anterior pituitary and the posterior pituitary.*

The scientific terms in this passage look as awkward as they are difficult to pronounce. But they need not be insurmountable obstacles. Notice the words and phrases you do recognize—"helps control heartbeat," "a small gland," "connected," and "has two portions." Using these few words alone, you can come up with a reasonable paraphrase of the passage:

"One gland, the hypothalamus, helps control your heartbeat. A small gland, the pituitary, has two parts."

If the question requires you to know more, you can at least begin with this foundation.

3. **Finally, if the passage topic is too difficult to paraphrase, try to answer these essential questions as you read: What is the author's purpose? What is the author's method?** Consider this passage from "Big Money and Politics" by Donald L. Barlett and James B. Steele.

> *It was just your typical piece of congressional dirty work when the House and Senate passed the District of Columbia Appropriations Act. You might think that would be a boring piece of legislation. You would be wrong. For buried in the endless clauses authorizing such spending items as $867 million for education and $5 million to promote the adoption of foster children was Section 6001: Superfund Recycling Equity. It had nothing to do with the District of Columbia, nor appropriations, nor equity as it is commonly defined. Instead Section 6001 was inserted in the appropriations bill by Senator Trent Lott of Mississippi, the Senate majority leader, to take the nation's scrap-metal dealers off the hook for millions of dollars in potential Superfund liabilities at toxic-waste sites.*

Anyone could get lost in the numbing numbers and "governmentese" such as *Superfund* and *equity*. But perhaps we can tease out a simple story beneath the obfuscation. The authors' purpose appears to be disabusing us of certain notions or, in other words, revealing to us the true workings of our elected officials. Furthermore, the authors are trying to demonstrate that point by showing us that the title of a piece of legislation (the "Superfund Recycling Equity") is misleading or even false. And voila! If you can reason that far, you probably know all you need to know about that passage.

Difficult? Not on your life.

Reading Fiction

The Hit Man's early years are complicated by the black bag that he wears over his head. Teachers correct his pronunciation, the coach criticizes his attitude, the principal dresses him down for branding preschoolers with a lit cigarette. He is a poor student. At lunch he sits alone, feeding bell peppers and salami into the dark slot of his mouth. In the hallways, wiry young athletes snatch at the black hood and slap the back of his head. When he is thirteen he is approached by the captain of the football team, who pins him down and attempts to remove the hood. The Hit Man wastes him. Five years, says the judge.

Welcome to the fun house. If the passage above seems a bit strange, brace yourself. One-fourth of the passages in the Critical Reading test are taken from fiction, just like the one above from a story by T. Coraghessan Boyle. Reading fiction is anything but straightforward.

The reader uses imagination to enter into the work and remain absorbed in it. He or she expects to have an aesthetic and emotional experience. The reader of fiction also assumes that the work has a unity, that is, everything is interrelated. If a suitcase shows up early on, you can be sure someone will eventually be taking a trip.

The fictional passages on the SAT exam require a different approach than the other kinds of passages:

1. **Read for the story, not the structure.** Unlike science passages, fiction doesn't always stick to a rigidly organized struc-

ture. In order to figure out what's going on and answer the questions, you're going to have to concentrate on what's happening among the characters.

For example, in the story "The Hit Man," we meet several characters including the Hit Man himself, a coach, a football captain, and a judge. Clearly, we should focus our attention on the Hit Man—the other characters are only there to help reveal aspects of his nature. And that nature is a bit mysterious. Why does he wear a black mask? Does he think he's Zorro? Is the black mask simply a metaphor? That is, does the Hit Man really wear a mask to school (not likely) or is it an artistic way for the writer to tell us this person keeps his inner feelings hidden?

2. **Read critically.** The SAT questions are going to ask you to go beneath the surface of the narrative, so ask yourself questions as you read. How do the characters feel about each other? What is the narrator's main concern?

   In our story the characters only interact to the extent that they oppose or antagonize the Hit Man. What is the author concerned about? Why do others dislike the Hit Man? Why is he so unlikable? Does he resent this treatment? There are no fast and easy answers to these questions, but we're not looking for facts. We're looking instead for puzzles. What issues does the author want us to ponder? What mysteries does he want us to explore?

3. **Note the author's language.** Many of the SAT questions are going to ask you why the author chose certain words or expressions. As you read, keep asking yourself the significance of the language the author uses.

   Again, let's look at "The Hit Man." It's noteworthy that none of the characters is given a name. Everyone is identified by his or her role, or at least one narrow aspect of that role—teacher, coach, captain. What might this suggest about the

> author's approach? That covers the nouns, now what about the verbs? The passage apparently took place years ago and yet is told in present tense. What might this tell us about the author's intent? Is the author reinforcing the idea that whatever happened to the Hit Man in the past is still affecting him in the present?

The real challenge for you in the fiction section is to read, in Thomas Foster's phrase, *like a professor*. How does a professor read? According to Foster, she relies on memory (who does this character remind me of and where have I seen this story before?), symbol (everything can be a symbol—but of what?), and pattern (man versus nature, boy meets girl, or, as Leslie Nielsen states it in *The Naked Gun*, "Same old story. Boy finds girl. Boy loses girl. Girl finds boy. Boy forgets girl. Boy remembers girl. Girl dies in tragic blimp accident over the Orange Bowl on New Year's Day.").

Read like a professor and you'll be ready to teach the class.

Come to Your Senses

We often miss the obvious because we dismiss easily. Study the poem below:

l(a

le
af
fa

ll

s)
one
l

iness

When E. E. Cummings published this poem in 1958, the reviews were worse than those for the movie *Gigli*. Really. The critics thought it was stupid. According to Brown University professor Barry A. Marks, it looked "more like a picture of the Washington Monument or a telephone pole than a poem."

So why did Marks feel that the poem deserves our attention. Although the letters seem to have collided and the entire poem is less than a complete sentence, Cummings sees what we do not. If you remove the parenthetical thought, what remains is the word "loneliness."

l

one
l

iness

Our eyes now see what Cummings saw. The word "loneliness" reminds us of how alone we are by repeating one-one-one. As Cummings teaches us, the letter "el" doubles as the figure "1." This repetition of meaning was always in the word "loneliness," but we didn't see it until Cummings split the word for us.

In understanding works of literature, don't forget the importance of your senses. Writers, especially poets, occasionally place words on the page as if they were actors on a stage. You must recognize the "actor's blocking" to fully interpret the meaning.

Your hearing matters, too. Welsh poet Dylan Thomas loved the sounds of words. He was known to choose a particular word because it pleased his ear—what it actually meant in the context of

the poem was secondary. To appreciate some of his poems, therefore, they must be read aloud.

As for your sense of smell, listen to almost any of the rhyming hip-hoppers that are so popular today. Now hold your nose. You may think, of course, that criticism is unfair. What do you think the average test maker would say about most of the things you believe are "cool"? As we suggested earlier: open your eyes. The irony is visible everywhere.

I'd rather learn from one bird how to sing than teach ten thousand stars how not to dance.

—E. E. Cummings

TEST STRATEGIES

When you're on the Titanic, *you load the lifeboats. You don't stop to yell at the iceberg.*
—Patricia Heaton, "Everybody Loves Raymond"

Think of the SAT as an iceberg. Think of the following ten strategies as your lifeboats.

Be the Test Maker

After all, what is reality anyway?
Nothing but a collective hunch.
—Lily Tomlin
Search for Signs of Intelligent Life in the Universe

OK, earning a high verbal score isn't exactly *Zen and the Art of Critical Reading*. But you need to stop thinking as a test taker and start thinking as a test maker. If you could crawl inside the brain of the average test maker, you wouldn't find the next Ozzie Osbourne. You would find, instead, someone who is positive, patriotic, politically correct. What does that mean to you? You should give serious consideration to answers that reflect those qualities.

Be careful, though, of assuming too much. In his book *Sex, Drugs, and Cocoa Puffs*, Chuck Klosterman reveals the results of a study he conducted on the effects of patriotism. He sent out a mass e-mail to his acquaintances. In the e-mail he gave everyone two potential options for a hypothetical blind date. The respondents were instructed to pick whom they'd prefer. The first candidate was described as "attractive and successful." The second candidate was said to be "attractive, successful, and extremely patriotic." No other details were given.

Are you surprised to learn that just about everyone responded by selecting the first individual? Klosterman's point is that many of us are suspicious of the "too patriotic." E-mail respondents compared the second individual to Ted Nugent and Patrick Henry. One said that patriotic people weren't smart. The lesson for you? Don't go overboard.

Two Self-Evident Truths

1. **The average test maker is just a little bit afraid.** Do you actually believe that the College Board wants to argue about which of their answers are correct? Test makers can't afford to be second-guessed by thousands of enraged students who provide plausible alternative answers. Test makers, therefore, tend toward the obvious answer, the unarguable answer. You should too.

2. **Don't outsmart yourself.** The SAT does not reward the "star" of classroom discussions: the meaning-behind-the-meaning kid, the clever kid, in short, anyone with a personality.

Ah, the Humanity (etc.)

I had always planned on going to Columbia . . .
but they had tests to get in.
—Jon Stewart, "The Daily Show"

This just in for all of you fake news show hosts of the future: you still have to take tests. Although the SAT now has shorter passages (about one hundred words long), the longer passages remain largely unchanged. The longer passages range from four hundred to eight hundred fifty words and include nonfiction selections from humanities, social studies, and natural sciences, as well as the specified fiction selection. At this writing, the possibility of paired passages still lurks in those oval heads of the test makers. You would read two paragraphs of about two hundred words each with four questions based on the two passages and the relationship between the passages.

Pay special attention to the following discussion of these longer passages. Each type of passage offers a unique challenge.

Ah, the Humanity

These passages are usually about art, literature, or philosophy. The focus is less on facts, more on inference. Consider what columnist Dave Barry has to say about the history of painting:

> *After the Mother and Child Phase came the Enormous Naked Women Eating Fruit Phase, which was followed by the Just Plain Fruit with No Women of Any Kind Phase and the Famous Kings and Dukes Wearing Silly Outfits Phase. All of the phases were part of the Sharp and Clear School of painting, which means that even though the subjects were boring, they were at least recognizable. The Sharp and Clear School ended with Vincent Van Gogh, who invented the Fuzzy but Still Recognizable School and cut off his ear. This led to the No Longer Recognizable at All School, and finally to the Sharp and Clear Again but Mostly Just Rectangles School, which is the school that is popular today, except at shopping malls.*

Now no one would accuse Barry of worrying about facts, but you can infer a thing or two from his insights. You won't find much in the way of great art at shopping malls, for example.

The most important thing to remember when reading these questions: *slow down*. Because some of the questions are based on inferences, you have to think about the implications of what you are reading. The good news is that these passages are almost always politically correct and positive. You are not likely to read a passage from an author asserting that Sir Laurence Olivier was overrated as an actor. Respond accordingly.

The SAT has been criticized in the past for insensitivity to minorities. If you come across a passage that discusses a minority issue, you can expect kid-glove treatment. In the SAT world, everything is beautiful in its own way.

To focus your thinking, you may want to jot down a few notes in the margin. (See Strategy 5 for suggestions.) If you can't separate the inferences, your hopes of answering the questions correctly could go up in flames.

And you don't want to be the next Hindenburg-er.

Houston, We Have a Passage

In a graduation talk for the UNC School of Information and Library Science, Martin Dillon's calculations demonstrated how trends and statistics can be dangerous. Evidently, the number of Elvis impersonators grew from 51 in 1981 to almost 15,000 in 1995. Dillon says, "If that trend continues, there will be some 50,000,000 Elvis impersonators in the U.S. alone by the year 2015. In the graduating class of that year, every 5th or 6th student would be an Elvis impersonator."

Elvis is not the only one who wants to leave the building. A science passage can be intimidating to anyone. Calculations discussed may be mind-boggling. The scientific jargon is often confusing. Fortunately, choosing the correct answer rarely depends on understanding a particular scientific term, and the calculations only matter on the Math section.

Any confusing scientific term will usually be explained in the sentences before and after it. For example, a question about "quarks" might seem difficult until you study that part of the passage that explains what a quark is. Since you have scanned the questions first (see Strategy 4), circle the word as you read the passage so you can find it later.

> *Of the several hundred subatomic particles out of which physicists tell us all matter is made, the quark is the most evasive, the most piquing, and the most basic—so small as to have no size and so simple as to have no internal structure. Of course nobody's managed to shake a quark loose for closer inspection (the most they've been able to do is to hit a few over the head with beams of electrons), but that hasn't stopped scientists from insisting that quarks, like black girl groups of the Sixties, usually travel in threes and carry electrical charges. . . .*
>
> —Judy Jones and William Wilson, *An Incomplete Education*

Remember: the answers to most of these questions are based on the facts in the passage. Rarely do you have to address the inferences in the passage. And, Science marches on.

History Retreats Itself

"To be is to do." Socrates

"To do is to be." Jean-Paul Sartre

"Do be do be do." Frank Sinatra
—Kurt Vonnegut Jr.

Here's to revisionist thinking! You've finally stumbled onto those questions of mass destruction that you knew were there all the time.

In the following passage, Robert Benchley describes what has become a tense, and sometimes confusing, part of most public meetings: "The Treasurer's Report."

Now, in connection with reading this report, there are one or two points which Dr. Murnie wanted brought up in connection with it, and he asked me to bring them up in connec—to bring them up.

In the first place, there is the question of the work which we are trying to do up there at our little place at Silver Lake, a work which we feel not only fills a very definite need in the community but also fills a very definite need—er—in the community. I don't think that many members of the society realize just how big the work is that we are trying to do up there. For instance, I don't think that it is generally known that most of our boys are between the age of fourteen. We feel that, by taking the boy at this age, we can get closer to his real nature—or a boy has a very real nature, you may be sure—and bring him into closer touch not only with the school, the parents, and with each other, but also the town in which they live, the country to whose flag they pay allegiance—and to the—ah—(trailing off) town in which they live.

Although what happens in public meetings is an important part of our history, these passages will generally be about a historical trend or period. The historian's interpretation and supporting examples are the source of the questions. Mark on the passage when you come across this interpretation and the beginning of each example (see also Strategy 5). A simple "I" and "E" would serve this purpose. You can expect the historian to reference conflicting opinions. You probably will be asked a question about this other "disagreeable" historian as well. You might place a "C" next to this argument.

Tell Me a Story

These fiction passages are the most enjoyable to read. You may find yourself saying, to borrow the unbridled enthusiasm of "The Daily Show's" Jon Stewart, "It's smile-tastic. It's tickle-riffic." Then again, maybe not.

But all was not play at the University of Minnesota. Now I began classes, and that was work—the good, satisfying work of learning.

I shall always remember the first class I attended. It was a class in sociology. I took a seat in the front row and spread my paper and pencils neatly on my desk. Turning to my brother students, I smiled friendlily. They threw lighted matches at me in a demonstration of good fellowship. Then the venerable white-haired professor entered the room. He advanced to the lectern at the head of the class. Putting on his pince-nez, he surveyed us for a moment. "Jeez," he said, "they get crumbier every year."

We laughed appreciatively.

In *Barefoot Boy with Cheek*, the author Max Shulman has his hero Asa Hearthrug laugh in the face of possible disaster. You, too, want to remain upbeat. So here is some advice about a fiction passage: don't rush through it. The questions will certainly address style and tone. You must be more aware of nuances in a fiction passage.

Warning: Do not read too much into your interpretation. You will not be rewarded for originality. Figure out the figurative language, but avoid overthinking your answers.

Two's a Crowd

The debate over including paired passages on the SAT continues. Therefore, you should be prepared to tackle them just in case. Questions following paired passages are in the same order as the passages. In other words, it makes sense to read the first passage and then answer the questions that are specific to the first passage. Next, read the second passage and answer the appropriate questions for that passage. Finally, answer the questions that deal with both passages. By the time you get to the last few questions, the "relationship" between the passages should be much clearer.

Warning: Do not read both passages before beginning the questions. Attack one passage at a time.

The Practice Passages section in this book will help you prepare for these questions.

You're out of my mind. Guess that makes two of us.

—John Gorka, *Out of My Mind*

Mo, Hairy, and Curly Context

Moe: *Quiet!*
Larry: *I'm sorry, Moe. Please forgive me.*
Curly: *I'm trying to think but nothing happens.*

When you take the SAT, nothing happens more often than it does on reruns of "Seinfeld." This Strategy, on the other hand, gives you something to think about faster than you can say, "Hey Moe!" Generally, the questions on the Critical Reading section fall into three Stooge-like categories.

1. Mo

These questions ask you about the "more," or the "Mo," of the passage, if you will. Some prep books call these the "Big Idea" or "Main Idea" questions.

> *I don't know. I mean, isn't Jake's impotence more about that generation's loss of faith in love?*
> —Rory, "Gilmore Girls"

In her English class at Yale, Rory defends her interpretation of Ernest Hemingway's novel *The Sun Also Rises*. Another student accuses Rory of ignoring the social context of underclass exploitation. What about World War I? Proving it's not always as easy as you think to find the bull in one of Hemingway's stories.

Fortunately, the "main idea" questions on the SAT are a little less debatable.

See if you can find Mo in the following passage:

> *If you really want to know what people in the United States are thinking about, you should write a letter to the editor. If you don't have time, National Public Radio's humorist Ian Shoales will do it for you. Here is an excerpt from one such letter that will please anyone regardless of political bent.*
>
> *"I realize this won't get printed in your so-called newspaper. The (Leftist, Conservative) slant is a disgrace to all (real Americans, taxpayers, our unborn children). Still I must urge everyone to (register to vote, write your Congressman, vote No on Prop 17) or we might not have (another four years, streetlights, a tomorrow).*
>
> *"As a (taxpayer, lifelong Democrat, home owner) I (view with alarm, am frightened by, am angered by) our (foreign policy, domestic policy, bleeding-heart environmentalists). Are we living in (a welfare state, Nazi Germany, a fool's paradise)?"*

You don't have to be in paradise to find the main idea in this passage. Shoales's willingness to write a letter for you is expressed near the beginning, the usual location for Mo. Some main ideas, however, are found later in the passage.

> *Tracy Ullman phones car dealers in Baltimore and comparison shops. Gary Oldman plays tapes on the freeway and ponders the uncanny congruities between Lee Harvey Oswald and Yogi Bear. Barbara Hershey tools through the Louisiana swamps and climbs ashore now and then for a chat.*
>
> *All these slightly undignified enterprises are dramatic research, simply the lengths to which some actors will go to find and perfect an acceptable accent.*

In this passage, Judith Shulevitz of the *New York Times* writes about the preparation process for some actors. The Mo is contained in the second paragraph following the examples discussed in the first paragraph. In the second paragraph, you learn that research to find an acceptable accent can be slightly undignified. The Mo.

2. Hairy

These questions can be trickier. The hairy part is finding the answer in the details of the passage. The hard questions are the ones where the answer is not apparent or, worse yet, hidden. You read more effectively when you read actively. Continually ask yourself: how do the supporting ideas link back to the main idea, the Mo? Sometimes that relationship is self-evident.

The young James Thurber, who later gained recognition as a cartoonist and humorist, struggled to win the approval of his editor. After the editor instructed Thurber to write short, dramatic leads, he produced the following:

> *Dead. That's what the man was when they found him with a knife in his back at 4:00* P.M. *in front of Riley's saloon at the corner of 52nd and 12th streets.*

In this passage, Riley's saloon is a detail. In fact, all of the information about the crime scene could be described as supporting details. What it takes to write a dramatic lead is the implied main idea.

When you attack the longer passages, finding the details that answer a particular question can be more challenging. A question may ask you to draw an inference from a detail provided.

> *In* Life on the Mississippi, *Mark Twain, writing in 1874, observed that the lower part of the Mississippi River had been*

shortened 242 miles during the past 176 years—a little more than a mile and a third each year.

From the details provided above you could infer that the Mississippi River would continue to shorten (unless measures were taken to change the course of history). If you read on, though, you discover that Twain's inferences are strikingly different from yours.

. . . any calm person who is not blind or idiotic can see that in the Old Oolithic Silurian Period, just a million years ago next November, the Lower Mississippi River was upward of one million three hundred thousand miles long . . . And by the same token any person can see that seven hundred and forty-two years from now the Lower Mississippi will be only a mile and three-quarters long.

Be careful. Don't assume too much, too quickly. And avoid the trap of trying to remember every single detail. In the past, more than two-thirds of the Critical Reading questions were hairy. These kinds of detail questions often refer to a specific line or paragraph. Fortunately, you can get the needed experience in finding details by completing the Practice Passages in this book.

3. Curly Context

Words are loaded pistols.
—Jean-Paul Sartre

Existentialism aside, Vocabulary in Context questions are the ones to unload first if you are running short on time. Sometimes the definition is fairly self-evident. The correct definition curls around the word to comfort you during your moment of need. Often, though, the test makers serve up a word with multiple definitions. You are given correct definitions for the word, but only one of those definitions works in context. You know the specific context because you will be given a line reference.

Warning: Don't rely on the common meaning for any word. The test makers will usually have a secondary definition among the choices. Just because an answer is true doesn't make it correct. For example, if you are asked about the word "skin," you might immediately think "epidermis." But the correct choice might be another meaning for that same word. As in, there's more than one way to skin a test maker.

Here are two examples to help you:

1. The words that curl around the term *Greek Chorus* state explicitly what you need to know.

    Greek plays were written in verse, like poetry, but the verse was close to the patterns of normal speech. The lines were spoken in unison by a chorus of people. The Greek Chorus consisted of members of the local population, and participation was considered a civic duty, much as voting is today.

2. Not all of the Vocabulary in Context questions, though, are that obvious.

    In the book *Weird Wide Web*, authors Erfert Fenton and David Benton speculate on why there are so many web pages devoted to Spam. They wonder: "Is Hormel's canned meat product perhaps a metaphor for the Internet itself—made up of diverse elements, ubiquitous, and virtually indestructible?"

    In this passage, the word *ubiquitous* means

A. divergent
B. omnipresent
C. carnivorous
D. cyberspace
E. imperishable

You can eliminate the wrong choices fairly easily. An author is unlikely to repeat synonyms in a sentence structured to list different characteristics. Therefore, you can eliminate A (divergent) and E (imperishable). They are synonyms for the words *diverse* and *indestructible* that are already a part of the list. The choice D (cyberspace) is the wrong part of speech (and it makes no sense in that sentence). Choice C (carnivorous) is there to fool you. The passage is about Spam. The Internet, however, is hardly a meat-eating entity. At least, not yet. The correct answer is B (omnipresent). The Internet is seemingly present everywhere. Watch out.

(conk) Woo woo woo woo woo woo woo woo woo woo, nyuk nyuk nyuk nyuk (bonk)

—Curly of "The Three Stooges"

The Questions Are the Answers

I have potential. Like I'm reading Moby Dick *and I'm not even halfway through and I can already tell you the ending. The whale is a robot. . . . Here's something I did not know. They number every page.*
—Michael Kelso, "That '70s Show"

In one study, every state with an average of math and verbal scores of 510 or above also had an average high temperature in January of less than 42 degrees. Does that mean you should be on the phone to your local meteorologist?

Probably not. Although the meteorologist would be a better bet than Kelso (unless, of course, you're in Wisconsin). You should, instead, consider the following four suggestions:

1. Scan Can

You should scan the passages to focus your mind. Simply skim quickly for now. The purpose of this skimming is to find a topic that interests you. Begin with that passage. The higher your level of interest is, the stronger your start will be. If none of the topics grab you, then it's time for mind games. Convince yourself that you are fascinated by the subject matter. You would be surprised how revved-up you can get reading a scientific passage disproving the alternative hypothesis that the average raven is "clever"—especially if you are familiar with Monty Python's hypothesis that a "clever sheep" is dangerous. Let your mind be your friend.

2. Speed Kills

Aoccdrnig to rscheearch at an Elingsh uinervtisy, it deosn't mttaer in what oredr the liteers in a wrod are, the olny iprmoetnt tihng is that the frist and lsat liteer are in the rghit pclae. The rset can be a toatl mses and you can sitil raed it wouthit a porbelm. Tihs is bcuseae we do not raed ervey lieter by itslef but the wrod as a wlohe and the biran fguiers it out aynawy.

—Phil Proctor, *Funny Times*

Some teachers contend that readers with the best comprehension are usually fast readers. The argument is based on the assumption that slow readers are more easily distracted. Daydream city, as it were. A more important concern, though, is how carefully you read the Critical Reading passages.

In the movie *Reuben, Reuben*, the subject of speed-reading is raised. Academy Award nominee Tom Conti—who portrays a drunken, but brilliant poet—says that he would pay someone to teach him to read his favorite books as slowly as possible. Clearly, the poet in this film wants to savor every word.

Although you don't have time for much savoring, you should read as carefully as you can *and* still finish within the constraints of the exam.

3. Questions First

As you confront each new passage, read the questions first. Just the questions, not the answers. Too many conflicting answers can lead to information overload. In the middle of an important sentence, you don't want to find yourself wondering, "What was choice C anyway?"

You want increased focus rather than increased confusion. Some prep books disagree with this advice. These books argue that you may become so preoccupied with searching for answers that you will fail to get the overall meaning of the passage. The best option for you is to try both ways on the Practice Passages in this book. Then stick with the system that works for you.

We recommend reading the questions first because reading comprehension is a two-step process: (1) perceiving and organizing information, and (2) connecting that information to what you already know. Your success in relating any information will increase if you have a frame of reference. The questions are that frame of reference. And those same questions should help you organize your thinking as you read through the passage.

Always remember that reading is an active process. Anticipate ideas. Your purpose is to actively search for the information you need to answer the questions you have already scanned. Have those questions in mind as you begin reading the passage. The search is about understanding. Don't worry about memorizing. Memorization is too time-consuming.

Tip: Unlike the rest of the SAT, Critical Reading questions are not in order of increasing difficulty. If you are running short of time, do the vocabulary in Curly context questions first, the Mo questions next, and the Hairy questions last.

4. Play the Odds

I used to be a gambler. But now I just make mental bets.
That's how I lost my mind.
—Steve Allen

How much would you pay for all the secrets of the Universe? OK, what if we throw in the odds of guessing on the SAT? But wait. What if we send you an ice crusher? The truth is that you should guess. That is, if you can eliminate one wrong answer.

The guessing penalty is really a wrong-answer penalty. We can't tell you what X is but we can do simple fractions. When you guess

wrong on one of the Critical Reading questions, you lose one-fourth of a point (unless they revise the rules—be sure to check before you take the test). The test makers are trying to discourage you from randomly selecting correct answers.

What does this mean to you? Well, if you can eliminate one of the answer choices, you now have a one-in-four chance of answering each question correctly. Theoretically, you should be able to guess the correct answer at least once in four tries. Since you are losing only one-fourth point for every miss, it's worth your while to guess. If you can eliminate more than one incorrect answer choice, your odds improve significantly. Unless you are extraordinarily unlucky.

When making difficult choices, former CIA director James Woolsey has his own way of determining the odds. Woolsey recalls the advice of the Damon Runyan character Harry the Horse. Runyan, a newspaperman in the 1920s, had Harry give this advice to gamblers: "Nothin' what depends on humans is worth odds of more than 8 to 5."

Context Messaging

To read between the lines was easier than to follow the text.
—Henry James

You don't have to read between the lines to know that students' reading skills have barely improved over the last decade. Clearly, few students are illiterate; too many, however, are "aliterate." These aliterate students can read, but they don't. And when they do, they are not fully engaged in the process. Such recalcitrance can affect how you approach those questions that refer you to specific words or lines in a passage. Read the following passage and answer the question that follows.

In 1951, Oliver Brown, an African-American railroad worker from Topeka, Kansas, sued the city of Topeka for preventing his daughter from attending a local all-white school. Eight-year-old Linda Brown was forced to ride a bus for five miles when there was a school only four blocks from her home. The case, which went all the way to the Supreme Court (*Brown v. Board of Education*), challenged the constitutionality of an 1896 ruling, *Plessy v. Ferguson*. In *Plessy*, the court had decided that segregation was permissible as long as blacks and whites had access to "separate but equal" facilities.

Thurgood Marshall and his team of lawyers, though, presented evidence demonstrating that "separate but equal" was a logical impossibility. There could be no such thing as "separate but equal" facilities when society was arranged unequally.

In a 9–0 landmark decision, the Supreme Court ruled that segregated facilities degraded minorities and prevented them from having equal educational opportunities. As Chief Justice Earl Warren wrote, "Separate educational facilities are inherently unequal." *Plessy* was overturned. Although the *Brown* decision applied only to education, it inspired minorities to seek rights in other fields, and it became a turning point in the civil rights movement.

Question: In lines 7–9, the importance of *Plessy* is addressed. The Supreme Court decision in *Brown v. Board of Education* affected this 1896 ruling by

A. challenging the constitutionality of *Plessy v. Ferguson*
B. becoming a turning point in the civil rights movement
C. changing "separate but equal" facilities
D. overturning *Plessy v. Ferguson*
E. improving public transportation in the South

Test makers can be tricky. If you skim the passage quickly or look only at lines 7 and 8, you might be tempted to choose A. The answer is true, but is it the best choice of the five? Later in the passage, you learn that the Supreme Court overturned *Plessy*. Ask yourself: does challenging the constitutionality of a ruling have a greater effect than overturning that ruling? No. Therefore, the correct answer is D. You could have quickly eliminated choices B and E because they don't deal specifically with *Plessy*. And choice C is simply not true.

Whenever the question refers you to specific lines in a passage, read the lines before and after to avoid such trickery. Stay engaged even if you find the subject matter of no interest to you. In the passage about *Brown v. Board of Education*, for example, you can heighten your interest by pretending that you really are Thurgood Marshall. And you have the opportunity to change this country for the better, but first you have to understand all of the facts of the case. An eight-year-old girl is depending on *you*.

In other words, no matter what a passage is about, you should invest yourself in what is at stake. Make the outcome matter to you, and the outcome will be better for you.

Two Suggestions to Make That Investment Pay Off

1. **Be Noteworthy.** Taking notes on the passage can help some students. The simple act of noting a significant idea makes the next idea clearer for them. Circle important words. Underline key concepts. Comprehension, after all, depends upon understanding each preceding thought. But you have to be efficient. Develop an abbreviation code that works for you. You are not trying to write a book in the margins of the paper. You are merely highlighting what you hope will help you choose correct answers later.

   In *Parade*, Marilyn vos Savant discusses the potenial disadvantage of relying on such markings. Vos Savant says, "Some top students highlight elementary information; others note arcane material; still others mark abstruse sections; plenty make markings as idiosyncratic as their personalities."

   As always, time yourself on the Practice Passages. How much does it slow you down to make markings? Do those markings improve your ability to answer the questions correctly?

2. **Be Handy.** Once you've selected an answer, return to the place in the passage where you found the necessary information. Actually put your finger on that spot. Using your finger in this way decreases the chances that your fertile imagination is

> coming into play. Too often, the pressure of the moment takes over. The knowledge you brought to the testing site predisposes you to make certain choices. Your biases cut loose. You can't quite remember the words to the song that is stuck in your head.

Find the correct answer in the passage, not in the "Well, I've always thought" corner of your cerebrum, cerebellum, or medulla oblongata. When the SAT test is finally over, you don't want to say, "And that's all folks," like some Elmer be-Fudd-led.

The Night Before the Night Before

When a normal person goes to sleep they do not enter dream sleep for maybe 90 minutes after falling asleep. When narcoleptics like myself fall asleep we enter dream sleep right away. I am still awake when I begin to dream and I experience my dreams as hallucinations. Believe me, they are very, very real. If I dream that I got bit, I can feel it.

—Melody Zarnke, forty-five years old

In *Esquire*'s book *What It Feels Like*, one woman describes her narcolepsy. For some reason, the editors at *Esquire* did not include what it feels like to take the SAT. Strangely, though, the nightmarish qualities of the SAT are remarkably similar to what the woman reveals. And your understanding of sleep patterns can make a significant difference in your ability to perform well on the test.

Harvard medical researchers have concluded that a good night's rest consolidates memory. Furthermore, any successful coach will tell you that performance in competition is enhanced by resting well the night before the night before. Lack of sleep always catches up with you on the second day. In other words: sleep—plus practice—makes perfect.

In one particularly memorable episode of the animated television show "King of the Hill," Peggy Hill preps to participate in a book discussion group. Her efforts include memorizing pertinent facts about famous authors from an encyclopedia.

> *All right. Kafka. Kafka born 1883. Wore glasses. Burdened by father. Loved to sleep in. Yes, Peggy, you are ready.*

Even if you are unfamiliar with Franz Kafka's *The Metamorphosis*, you don't want to wake up the morning before the SAT as a cockroach. And it's certainly not the time to sleep in. Wake up! Starbucks awaits.

Be Happy, Be Healthy

Increasing evidence shows that personality, stress, and social life can all influence your vulnerability to cold symptoms. Psychologist Sheldon Cohen of Carnegie-Mellon University in Pittsburgh compares it to kindergarten: those who "play well with others" are better off. What does this mean? Well, according to Marilyn Elias in *USA Today*:

DR. JEKYLL AND MR. COFFEE

- Happy, relaxed people are more resistant to illness than those who tend to be unhappy or tense. And when happy people do get sick, their symptoms are milder.
- The more extroverted a person is, the less likely he is to catch cold.
- The longer people live with bad stress, the more likely they are to catch colds.

As you know, an exercise program can improve your state of mind by reducing anxiety. Moreover, you will have more oxygen getting to your brain, and you will be better able to think and to concentrate. The extra energy you gain from regular physical preparation will help sustain you during the latter parts of the exam. If you take regular exercise breaks during your study periods before the exam, your productivity will increase. Endorphins are your friends. Don't exercise, though, right before going to bed. Such activity can make restful sleep difficult.

Finally, eat smart. Now is not the time to be a junk-food junkie. Consume the low-fat protein in fish, skinless poultry, beans, and legumes. Just say no to sugar and fat. These substances increase stress and lower immunity. Remember: Mom knows best. Ask her.

So all you really need to do is to change your entire personality. And make sure you get plenty of sleep the night before the night before.

Sweet dreams, slugabed.

Translate Questions into English

"Wheel of Fortune" was an important SAT prep for me.
—Mo Rocca, "The Daily Show"

In 1996, after thirteen successful years on "Wheel of Fortune," letter-turner Vanna White set a world record for the greatest quantity of apparel ever on television—5,500 outfits. A proud day for the entire White family. And what did she do on the show? Vanna White turned enough small boxes to reveal hidden letters that a discerning viewer would want to be disemvoweled.

But there is a lesson here. The hidden phrases that contestants must guess to win are quickly obvious to everyone in the audience and at home. Quick and obvious are good things, especially when you're under the pressure of a timed exam. Therefore, you should immediately translate all questions into words and phrases you recognize and understand. This translation is not always as easy as it sounds.

As a high school student, University of Chicago professor Austan Goolsbee discussed the potential for absurdity:

> *How does the SAT judge your academic promise? Well, if you can define words like* desuetude *and* lascivious, *then you have average potential. To rank at the top, you need to know words like* ouabain, *which is an African poison, or* schistosomiasis, *an endemic disease mentioned in the novel* Lord Jim. *I'll admit, such words may come in handy on a*

really boring date when you have nothing else to talk about, but do they accurately reflect learning potential?

The truth is that the College Board chooses words and passages that are intentionally unfamiliar. That makes sense. No student should have the advantage of having studied the material before the exam. Unfortunately, some obscure passages are steeped in language just as obscure.

Your task becomes, then, to translate that language into understandable ideas. In other words, *paraphrase.*

With a doff of the thinking cap to Edwin Newman's *On Language*, let's practice on three statements that lack clarity.

1. *In order to improve security, we request that, effective immediately, no employees use the above subject doors for ingress and egress to the building.*

In other words, don't open these doors.

2. *The older man became an experiencing person in my life, lending an aura to my developing personality of absolute rapport and communicatory relevance.*

The older man was sympathetic and understanding.

3. *The definition of net wage rate in equation (2) suggests that wage-rate changes are best parameterized by changes in u.*

Well . . . u are in big trouble . . . plus we all know how painful parameterizing can be.

There are, of course, other ways to get lost in the language "bewilderness." A critical reader should be aware of euphemisms. Writers sometimes substitute euphemisms for words that are harsh or distasteful. Euphemisms often avoid the truth, lack clarity, and are more evasive than helpful.

Pentagon officials are frequent winners of the "Doublespeak Award," which is given yearly to the individuals or groups that have done the most outstanding job of using language meant to "bamboozle and befuddle." Once, in the 1990s, the National Council of Teachers of English presented the award to the Defense Department for giving us an "armed situation"—not a war—in the Persian Gulf.

War is tough on words, according to the English teachers. The Gulf War was rich in euphemisms, says William Lutz, a Rutgers University professor and chairman of the organization's Committee on Public Doublespeak.

For instance, bombing attacks against Iraq in 1991 were "efforts," and warplanes were "weapon systems." When pilots were on missions, they were "visiting a site." Buildings were "hard targets" and people were "soft" ones. Bombs didn't kill. They "degraded," "neutralized," "cleansed," or "sanitized." Killing the enemy was termed "servicing the target."

The allies were also guilty as charged by the teachers. The government of Saudi Arabia, unable to accept U.S. female soldiers, called them "males with female features."

Understand Overstatements

So far, we've focused on reading the passages in the SAT exam. But there's something else that requires reading—the answers. Sometimes a careful reading of the answers could help you eliminate some contenders and leave the field clear for the winner.

Be on the lookout, for example, for overstatements ("everyone agrees," "she never does that," "all of us insist") and sweeping language that pushes aside any moderation or nuance. It's rare on the SAT that the correct answer would be so one-sided. Most of the passages are written by teachers or professors—people given to moderate, carefully considered opinions. Choices with extreme or exaggerated claims distort the real meaning of the passage.

In this passage, for example, on the *Lord of the Rings* movie trilogy, note answers B and D.

The basis of the movies is J. R. R. Tolkien's trilogy of Middle Earth books, themselves a reworking of similar ancient themes. For, in his writings, the scholarly Tolkien liberally lifted from myth, folklore, and ancient languages. The name "Middle Earth," for example, was either taken from Old English or from the Norse creation myth. The names of the dwarves, Gandalf, and other wizards were lifted from Snorri Sturluson's "Prose Edde," and Mordor, the evil enclave that Frodo Baggins must traverse to deliver the ring to Mount Doom, is Old English for "murder."

Question: Which of the following best explains how Tolkien wrote *Lord of the Rings?*

A. Tolkien recycles ancient mythology and religion.
B. The characters and settings come entirely from his imagination.
C. He plagiarized from many now forgotten works of folklore.
D. Virtually every character and place name in *Lord of the Rings* comes from Norse myths or Old English stories.
E. The author uses his imagination to give new life to figures from folktales and literature of the Middle Ages.

Both B and D are too sweeping to do justice to Tolkien's true method. The correct answer, in case you're keeping score, is E.

Just as SAT passages tend to express moderate, carefully constructed positions, they also tend to focus on specific topics and that means you can rule out answers that sound too general. Choices with the wrong scope are either too broad or narrow in focus—either they're too general for the passage, or they focus too much on the details. Remember Goldilocks?

The first bowl of porridge she tried was too hot, the second too cool, and only the third just right. That's what you're looking for in a correct answer—something not too hot or too cold. Easier said than done, perhaps.

Finally, you should be wary of answers that seem correct in every respect—except that they contradict the passage. Often on the SAT, you'll find answers that sound OK but don't answer the question at all, or worse yet, they say the exact opposite of the correct answer. These answers sound reasonable, but they just don't fit the passage.

Such answers may be more tempting than you might think. They often have all the elements of a correct answer, and in the right order, but they insert a tiny word such as "not" or "no" and completely subvert the real meaning of the passage. For example, suppose the passage in question was this:

> *In the 1990s, when gambling on college sports became a major attraction at Las Vegas casinos, the betting action topped $2 billion a year, and the NCAA basketball championship rivaled the Super Bowl as the single largest gambling event. More college athletes were involved in fixing games or wagering on college teams than in any of the decades before legalized gaming became popular.*

Your question might be: what is the author's position on college athletes and gambling?

A wrong, but compelling answer might be: "College athletes are prohibited from gambling by the NCAA." That statement is true, but it hardly fits the passage. Worse yet, consider this answer: "College athletes are no longer in jeopardy because sports betting has been legalized in Las Vegas."

Alas, not true of life, not true of the passage.

Read as a Writer

When author Anna Quindlen was in the eighth grade, she took a scholarship test for a convent school. The essay test began with the quotation:

It is a far, far better thing that I do, than I have ever done; it is a far, far better rest that I go to, than I have ever known.

In her book *How Reading Changed My Life*, Quindlen describes how she knew that the scholarship was hers. "How many times had I gone up the steps to the guillotine with Sydney Carton as he went to that 'far, far better rest' at the end of *A Tale of Two Cities*?"

Quindlen, of course, went on to win a Pulitzer Prize and to become a bestselling author. But her journey began with a love for reading books. Long before she ever plugged in a word processor, she had made reading "her home, her sustenance." And she ate book after book. You should do the same. Furthermore, you should live within the pages of each book. You, too, can find yourself on the steps "to the guillotine with Sydney Carton."

But for a far, far better rest, you should try to think as Dickens did. As Quindlen does today. Read as a writer. Writing teacher Donald M. Murray reminds us that "the woman who plays basketball watches the game differently than the people around her, in the bleachers." What Murray means is that you need to become involved in the text as if you were the writer. A writer will study the Critical Reading passages with a more critical eye.

Imagine the unwritten text before you. A writer must choose among a seemingly infinite number of words, scribbled notes, scattered memories, distracting thoughts, and so on. The writer takes those bits and pieces and puts them together to form meaning. If you approach each passage with the understanding that it once was an unwritten text, you have a better chance of deciphering the meaning of each phrase, sentence, and paragraph. You are, as Murray would argue, an archeologist sifting "through the refuse of an ancient civilization." You are searching for fragments of truth. Find those fragments and you can answer any question.

In the Foreword to the SAT Essay book in this series, Arthur Golden explains that context is everything. He states that a passage isn't beautiful "because of the writer's choice of words so much as because it draws together and draws upon, the material that comes before it." When you, as a reader, understand that those choices work collectively to create meaning, then you are well on your way to finding what is hidden. Study the following words of Seymour Glass, a character created by J. D. Salinger.

> *Certain heads, certain colors, and textures of human hair leave permanent marks on me. Other things too. Charlotte once ran away from me outside the studio, and I grabbed her dress to stop her, to keep her near me. A yellow cotton dress I loved because it was too long for her. I still have a lemon-yellow mark on the palm of my right hand. Oh, God, if I'm anything by a clinical name, I'm kind of a paranoic in reverse. I suspect people of plotting to make me happy.*

The Cliffs Notes interpretation would point out that certain things go unnoticed by most people. What else is there? Remember that Salinger made specific choices as a writer that can help you as a reader. You must, though, begin to think as a writer thinks. Look for the unexpected possibility. For example, consider two choices made for the Seymour Glass passage.

1. Why would Salinger have Seymour love a dress that was too long? Does this detail suggest the innocence of a female child?

2. Is it important that the dress is yellow? Does that color suggest a reason for a permanent mark, a scar?

When you ask those kinds of questions, you are thinking as Salinger might have—in context. The answers that Salinger would offer don't really matter now. Your reading life is richer already, just for the asking.

Be a Medi-Tater Tot

A man ought to read just as inclination leads him;
for what he reads as a task will do him little good.
—Samuel Johnson

Of course, Dr. Johnson never had to take the SAT. The prospect of this rite of passage might have convinced him to make an exception for our book. The triumph of experience over hope, he might say. In the "Introduction" to *The Best American Nonrequired Reading 2003*, the delightful Zadie Smith observes that the "task" of required reading is never done. She argues that "Tradition is a formative and immense part of a writer's world . . . but experiment is essential."

Smith makes an excellent point. While you are currently preparing to answer questions on the SAT, you are also preparing for a lifetime of reading. You should not let the forced nature of temporary SAT preparation sour you permanently. Make "experimenting" a part of your reading life and you will always know what Smith calls the "joy of nonrequiredness."

So start reading now.

Experiment

Dr. Tom Fischgrund's study of students who got perfect scores on the SAT found that those students read nearly twice as much as average academic achievers. Surprisingly, though, it didn't seem to matter much what they read. No "must-read" books emerged from the study. The key was to read a lot.

We suggest, however, that you choose books that challenge you and make you think. The more consideration you give to the ideas presented in a book, the more understanding you will have when asked difficult questions about those ideas. Read as much as you can the month before the exam. No matter what you read, you will improve your comprehension skills.

About a week before the SAT, take a timed, full-length practice test, and not just the Critical Reading section discussed in this book. This trial run will give you ample opportunity to assess what you still don't know and to take corrective measures. For the Critical Reading errors you have made, review the applicable parts of this book. Start resting two days before the test.

Tip: Cramming the night before the exam is not as beneficial as meditating.

> *And remember—always breathe. Even if I stop, you keep breathing out there, all right? Keep breathing. In and out. In and out. In and out.*
>
> —Christopher Durang, *Laughing Wild*

Although the woman speaking in Durang's play is trying to find a way to keep "laughing wild amid severest woe," her advice is meaningful to you—especially as you confront the severest woes of the SAT. Relaxation and visualization can help you increase your chances for success.

Relaxation

Find a quiet setting. Sit in a comfortable chair. Breathe. Breathe deeply. Fill your lungs with the pleasure of sweet air. Then exhale. Repeat. Sink lower into the chair. Close your eyes. Clear your mind. Let yourself begin to breathe easily and naturally.

If this exercise fails to relax you (or you find it silly), turn to professional help.

Perhaps the classic work on relaxation is based on studies at Boston's Beth Israel Hospital and Harvard Medical School. *The Relaxation Response* by Herbert Benson and Miriam Z. Klipper is a simple, mind-body approach to relieving stress. Also recommended is *The Relaxation & Stress Reduction Workbook* by Martha Davis et al. This 280-page workbook is jam-packed with specific techniques for the stressed-at-large.

Visualization

Once you are relaxed, you should begin to visualize succeeding on the SAT. Visualization is seeing images in your mind as vividly as possible. This technique is not magic. You are merely taking advantage of the natural process of thoughts. Your thoughts should create a matrix or a blueprint for your success. If we see in our imagination what we want, it is more likely to happen.

So after you are in a relaxed state of mind, concentrate on that image. See every detail; the institutional clock on the wall, the wooden desk, the number 2 pencils, the pink Mohawk haircut of the student sitting in front of you, the sounds, the smells—and not just from the student blocking your view. Try to feel your elation as you answer each question correctly. Know that joy now. Right now. Live in that moment. Trust your brain to respond.

Keep telling yourself, "I am relaxed. I can answer those questions." You may scoff at this advice but World Class athletes practice visualization. And it's not for fun. The athletes understand that picturing success increases their chances for success.

As Willy Loman said in Arthur Miller's play *Death of a Salesman*, "Attention must be paid."

PRACTICE PASSAGES

Chance favors the prepared mind.
—Louis Pasteur

On his MSNBC show "Hardball," Chris Matthews quoted Pasteur's observation about chance as a way of explaining his own good fortune in life. Good advice for you. Prepare your mind by practicing with the passages that follow.

Preparing for the Practice Passages

While you are practicing, take comfort in the fact that you don't have to study the 800-page book *G.O.A.T. (Greatest of All Time)*. This tribute to Muhammad Ali weighs seventy-five pounds and sells for $3,545. On the other hand, you might learn some important lessons from the life of Ali. Angelo Dundee, Ali's former trainer, reminds us: "You never get to go back in life." Therefore, make chance your friend. Prepare. Don't be the dope that gets roped.

Therefore, what can you expect when you reach the Critical Reading passages?

- **Length.** The passages come in three varieties: long, short, and paired. The long passages generally run from 400 to 850 words, and the short passages are usually from 100 to 250 words long. The paired passages, if included, are two short passages on a common theme; usually, the passages will present conflicting or contrasting points of view.
- **Content.** The passages are taken from four areas: the arts and humanities, social sciences, natural sciences, and fiction. They can vary in style and may include narrative, argumentative, or expository elements.
- **Number of questions.** You can expect to find as few as five or as many as thirteen questions following each passage. In the practice passages you will find here, we have limited our questions to one per short passage and two per long passage to help you focus your study (and prevent exhaustion).

- **Additional material.** The passages often come packaged with introductions and footnotes. Don't skip over these items: they help provide context for the passage and can sometimes help you find the right answer.

I know what you are going to ask and the answer is unknown.

Short Passages

Passage I

This passage was adapted from The Book of Lists 2 *by David Wallechinsky et al.*

Claude Pepper vs. George Smathers
U.S. Senatorial Primary Election (1950)

> At the start of the McCarthy era, Floridian Claude Pepper, one of the Senate's most outspoken liberals, was on the conservative's "hit list" along with many other senators. George Smathers lashed out with some typical right-wing invective—he called his opponent "the red pepper" and he launched a campaign to expose Pepper's secret "vices." Smathers disclosed that Pepper was a known "extrovert," his sister was a "thespian," and his brother a "practicing Homo sapien." Also, when Pepper went to college, he actually "matriculated." Worst of all, he "practiced celibacy" before marriage. Naturally, rural voters were horrified, and Pepper lost.

Question: Information provided in this passage would suggest which one of the following "slurs" was the most damaging to Claude Pepper's candidacy?

A. the red pepper
B. thespian
C. practicing Homo sapien

D. matriculated
E. practiced celibacy

Commentary

This question is challenging because all of the answer choices are true "slurs." You are given two clues, however, to suggest that the correct choice is A. The first clue is "At the start of the McCarthy era," that provides the historical perspective and the focus for the rest of the passage. Joseph McCarthy, a Wisconsin senator, was on a crusade to expose Communists and traitors. Therefore, calling Claude Pepper "the red pepper" would have been especially damaging at this time in history. The second clue is that "the red pepper" was listed first in the passage. The other "slurs" might be considered simply more—but lesser—examples. The phrase "worst of all" is tongue-in-cheek and not to be taken seriously.

....

Passage 2

In his foreword to the book Can You Find It?, *Dr. Michael McElroy, chair of the Department of Earth and Planetary Sciences at Harvard University, has concluded the following:*

The libraries of Harvard University alone contain over 11 million volumes. Assuming that each volume has about 150 pages, with about 400 words per page, we may calculate the store of wisdom at Harvard to run to approximately 660 billion words. If we assume that the accomplished reader can process about 50 words per minute, it is easy, for a skilled arithmetician at least, to estimate how long it would take to survey the material at Harvard. The answer is a staggering 25,000 years, and that does not allow time for sleep or other distraction.

Question: Dr. McElroy's arithmetical calculations

A. demonstrate that sleep and other distractions keep us from learning what we should
B. make it clear that processing 50 words a minute is not enough
C. are flawed because the number of volumes at Harvard's libraries keeps changing
D. prove the impossibility of knowing the store of wisdom at Harvard
E. would have different results at the University of Nebraska

Commentary

The correct choice is D. Again, you are challenged to select the best answer from among five choices that are essentially true. Remember, just because an answer is true doesn't make it correct or the best choice. Ask yourself, why would Dr. McElroy waste his time writing about any of the choices other than the "store of wisdom at Harvard?" Sometimes it's all about common sense.

. . . .

Passage 3

Movie review, "The Maria Problem," by Anthony Lane

When I arrived on a Friday night, an hour before the start of the sing-along version of *The Sound of Music*, the area around the cinema was packed. To be specific, it was packed with nuns. Many of them bore guitars. I was one of the few pathetic creatures who had not made the effort to come in costume. There were Nazis, naturally, plus a load of people who looked like giant parcels. I didn't get it. "Who are they?"

I said to a nun who has having a quick cigarette before the film. She looked at me with celestial pity and blew smoke. "Brown Paper Packages Tied Up with Strings," she replied. I am relieved, on the whole, that I missed the rugby team who piled into one screening as Girls in White Dresses with Blue Satin Sashes; on the other hand, it is a source of infinite sadness to me that I wasn't at the theater when a guy turned up in a skintight body costume in bright yellow; asked which character he was intended to represent, he explained that he was Ray, a Drop of Golden Sun.

Question: Which of the following best represents the tone of the passage?

A. mocking
B. admiring
C. sympathetic
D. sad
E. pitying

Commentary

Pitying (E) is the feeling the nun with the cigarette, not the narrator, expresses. When the narrator says he finds missing Ray, a Drop of Golden Sun, a source of infinite sadness (D), he is being sarcastic. The fact that the narrator can't figure out what some of the costumes represent helps us discard answer B (admiring). C (sympathetic) may be ultimately true of the narrator, but there's no evidence of it in this passage. The best answer, A (mocking), is shown in the narrator's phrase, "I was one of the few pathetic creatures," as well as his general attitude toward the amusing antics of these Julie Andrews fans.

Passage 4

Excerpt from My Losing Season *by Pat Conroy*

The lessons I learned while playing basketball for the Citadel Bulldogs have proven priceless to me as both a writer and a man. I have a sense of fair play and sportsmanship. My work ethic is credible and you can count on me in the clutch. When given an assignment, I carry it out to completion, my five senses lit up in concentration. I believe with all my heart that athletics is one of the finest preparations for most of the intricacies and darknesses a human life can throw at you. Athletics provide some of the richest fields of both metaphor and cliché to measure our lives against the intrusions and aggressions of other people. Basketball forced me to deal head-on with my inadequacies and terrors with no room or tolerance for evasion. Though it was a long process, I learned to honor myself for what I accomplished in a sport where I was overmatched and out of my league. I never once approached greatness, but toward the end of my career, I was always in the game.

Question: What is significant about the statement, "I was always in the game"?

A. that he was good enough that he didn't have to ride the bench
B. that he kept his team in games score-wise
C. that he always paid attention to what was happening on the court even if he wasn't playing
D. that he had internalized values that made him a better person
E. that he had developed a love for the game of basketball

Commentary

Conroy's statement, "I was overmatched and out of my league," tells you that A and B are not likely answers. That D is a better choice than C comes from the first four sentences that tell how Conroy has applied the lessons he learned from basketball to other areas of his life.

Passage 5

Excerpt from the article "Go North, Young Man" by Richard Rodriguez

Traditionally, America has been an east-west country. We have read our history right to left across the page. We were oblivious of Canada. We barely noticed Mexico, except when Mexico got in the way of our westward migration, which we interpreted as the will of God, "manifest destiny."

In a Protestant country that believed in rebirth (the Easter promise), land became our metaphor for possibility. As long as there was land ahead of us—Ohio, Illinois, Nebraska—we could believe in change; we could abandon our in-laws, leave disappointments behind, to start anew further west. California symbolized ultimate possibility, future-time, the end of the line, where loonies and prophets lived, where America's fads necessarily began.

Nineteenth-century real estate developers and twentieth-century Hollywood moguls may have advertised the futuristic myth of California to the rest of America, but the myth was one Americans were predisposed to believe. The idea of California was invented by Americans many miles away.

Question: Complete this sentence: Land became our metaphor for possibility because

A. there was such great opportunity for real estate development in California
B. advertising attracted attention
C. families could get away from their in-laws
D. people anticipated better opportunities if there was a chance to start anew
E. California symbolized America's fads

Commentary

People are ever optimistic that success is just over the next hill, therefore, D portrays the best answer. A and B may not have been true because communication was not that advanced. C would hardly be the answer because families needed each other to survive. E purports to symbolize loonies and prophets, not mainstream folks.

• •

Passage 6

Excerpt from the article "The Endless Hunt" by Gretel Ehrlich

A young Inuit friend asked if I had come to Greenland from California by dogsled. He had never traveled any other way and didn't realize that the entire world wasn't covered by ice. At age seven, he had never seen a car or a highway or been in an airplane, and he assumed the world was flat. He is part of a group of Polar Eskimos in northwest Greenland who still share in an ice-age culture that began more than 4,000 years ago, when nomadic boreal hunters began walking from Ellesmere Island across the ice to Greenland. Many of their ancient practices—hunting with harpoons, wearing skins, and traveling by dogsled—have survived despite modernizing influences that began at the turn of the century, when the explorer Robert Peary gave them rifles. The Arctic cold and ice have kept these hardy and efficient people isolated even today.

Question: The author's attitude toward the Inuit could best be described as

A. perplexed and appalled by their ignorance of modern technology
B. charmed by the innocence of their traditional culture
C. eager to share modernizing influences with them
D. determined to protect them from the modern world
E. convinced they are a heroic people in spite of their limitations

Commentary

A might be the response a less sympathetic narrator would have, but it is clear that this writer admires the Inuit. C is probably opposite from the author's real view—she celebrates how these ancient practices have "survived" despite modern influences. D comes close to the author's attitude but represents a much stronger position than she takes. B is probably true—the author appears amused at the seven-year-old boy's question—but it's not as important as E, the correct answer.

Long Passages

A. Natural Sciences

Political Pinocchios

This passage, adapted from the book Speech: Communication Matters, *discusses how technology can help us know when someone is lying.*

The purpose of debate is to determine the truth. But how can we tell if those politicians engaging in televised debates are being honest? Technology offers a new way to determine who is lying and who isn't.

A recently developed computer system can detect the little movements a person's facial muscles make when the person is displaying emotion. Smiling makes crow's-feet form around the eyes, for example, while frowning involves movements in forehead muscles. The system imposes a grid over a baseline black-and-white photograph of the subject's face when it is free from all expression. Any change in expression, even one that is very small or very fast, is recognized as a departure from baseline.

By analyzing the person's facial expressions, we can tell how that person truly feels, because facial expressions are hard to fake, even for experienced liars. Suppose a candidate is angered by a certain statement but wishes not to show that anger. According to a leading researcher, no matter how fast the candidate covers an angry frown with a smile, the computer system will detect the changing expression.

Of course, the process of refining facial-recognition systems continues. The Salk Institute for Biological Studies has mimicked the neural networks of the visual cortex. The 60 prototypical expressions used as program templates break facial expressions down into component movements. For example, the sixth template, called T6, encodes crinkling of the eyes, and an upturning of the lips is coded by the twelfth template. A smile is then a T6 combined with a T12.

However, hard engineering work lies ahead for any facial-recognition system. A system must be able to compensate for variable lighting and head positions. Improvements are also needed in identifying coordinated combinations of muscle movements.

What about the lie detector or polygraph? Isn't it just as effective? We might have trouble convincing politicians to agree to be hooked up to polygraphs during TV debates. But even if we could, we might not want to rely too heavily on the results.

Polygraphs use sensors to record changes in a person's respiration, heart rate, blood pressure, and skin conductance (how much sweat is being produced). The general idea is that a person who is lying will experience emotional stress. Emotional stress will produce certain bodily responses, such as increased heart rate and sweating.

This principle doesn't always hold up. Experienced liars may feel no emotional stress when they lie. Clever liars may be able to manipulate the test in various ways (for example, by taking a tranquilizer before testing). In either case, these people's bodily responses may indicate that they are not lying, even though they are. Also, people who are not lying may be experiencing a great deal of emotional stress during the test. They may be upset because they have been wrongfully accused. The bodily responses of these people may suggest that they are lying even though they aren't.

The new computer systems for detecting facial expressions may be harder to fool than the polygraph. As suggested earlier, the muscle movements involved in facial expressions are very difficult to control. Although a flash of anger or embarrassment may pass so quickly that the human eye cannot detect it, the computer will pick it up. So perhaps we can finally tell if those politicians are being honest—or just playing Pinocchio.

Question 1: You may infer from the passage that the facial-recognition system

A. can be fooled by covering an angry frown with a smile
B. makes measuring emotional stress more quantifiable
C. produces increased heart rate and sweating
D. is less effective than the polygraph test
E. compensates for all lighting and head variations

Commentary

The correct choice is B. The sixty prototypical templates tell you that the scientists are attempting to quantify emotions. A careful reading of the passage reveals that the other choices are just plain wrong. You can usually eliminate a choice like E because of the word "all." Beware of choosing answers expressed as absolutes.

Question 2: In line 35 the author uses the word "effective" to imply that

A. a clever liar can manipulate the polygraph
B. the polygraph is less likely to be used
C. experienced liars may feel no emotional stress
D. emotional stress may cause false-positive tests
E. all of the above

Commentary

The correct choice is E. If you skim the lines that surround the word "effective," you will immediately realize that more than one of the first four choices is correct. The moment that you know that at least two answers work, you can choose "all of the above."

• •

Speak, Robot

This passage, adapted from Glencoe Speech, *discusses one example of technology's increasing presence in our lives.*

When "Sesame Street's" Kermit the Frog won an honorary degree from Southampton College, Samantha Chie, a marine biology major, said, "Now we have a sock talking at our commencement. It's kind of upsetting." Clearly Chie was not impressed by Kermit's "Doctorate of Amphibious Letters."

Commencement speakers often create controversy. At Maryland's Anne Arundel Community College, one not entirely welcome commencement speaker felt nothing, because "he" was an "it": a 5-ft.-2-in.-tall, 175-lb. mobile machine loaded with a computer named, by its California manufacturer, Robot Redford.

Time magazine reports that the invitation originated with the dean, Anthony Pappas, who wanted to dramatize the high-tech transformation of the working world. Said Pappas: "This will call attention to the college's new unit in computer sciences and technology." Some among the 551-member class were miffed. "I don't like the idea," said Kimberly Roy, the student-government president. "It is not a human being like we are. We deserve more."

And that concern raises important questions. Can a robot be programmed to say something meaningful? Furthermore, does the programmer have something meaningful to say and was this robot the means to deliver that message? Not that night. C. Edward Scebold said, "For all the fuss and although the robot could have been programmed to speak, its voice was not loud enough to carry throughout the auditorium where commencement took place, so the speech was actually delivered by the robot's creator offstage while the audience looked at Robot Redford."

Although the machine's shortcomings provided a fitting anticlimax, the speech said, "You see, a robot is only an extension of the human body, and to meet the demands of the future, the human body will have to expand its energies. The computer doesn't replace the human mind, but increases the workload so we can continue to create and store knowledge."

Before the ceremony, the creator Bill Bakeleinkoff said: "As soon as he gets ten minutes into his speech, they'll forget he's a robot. Afterward they'll probably take him to the local malt shop and buy him new batteries."

The malt-shop trip was not in the offing, however. A plethora of stories discussed the implications of such technology. Educators debated the future of society. How can we re-educate ourselves to utilize technology we didn't devise and are not prepared to implement? What answers can computers provide to the problems facing education? Is there a risk of losing what makes us human?

Those who witnessed the commencement address were reminded of the inevitability of change. Still, some traditions were observed. Robot Redford, remotely controlled and made of fiberglass and aluminum, marched in the academic procession, but was not dressed in gown and mortarboard. "We didn't want to hoke it up," said Sara Gilbert, a spokesperson for the college.

Question 1: Which of the following best captures the meaning of the word "miffed" in line 17?

A. offended
B. surprised
C. not welcoming
D. not impressed
E. mortified

Commentary

The correct choice is A. You can figure this out from context. The next sentence begins with "I don't like the idea." That eliminates choices B (surprised) and E (mortified). Not liking the speaker does not suggest surprise or humiliation. Choices C and D have words that are used in other parts of the passage in ways that are not applicable in this context.

Question 2: Robot Redford's speech stated

A. that he didn't want to hoke things up
B. computers can help solve problems in education
C. the computer doesn't replace the human mind
D. that he had something meaningful to say
E. they'll forget he's a robot

Commentary

The correct choice is C. If you read the question closely, this one is easy. The only time the speech is quoted is in lines 31–36. The other choices are in the passage but are not a part of what the "speech stated."

B. Social Sciences

Navajo Code Talkers

This passage was adapted from the book Speech: Communication Matters. *It discusses the significant role that the Navajo Code Talkers played in World War II.*

During World War II, the United States Marines relied on the unique logic of the Navajo Code Talkers. Established in September of 1942, the Navajos created the first and only code that was never broken by the Japanese. The program was the result of a recommendation made by Mr. Philip Johnston.

Johnston, the son of a missionary to the Navajo tribe, was fluent in the language. He argued that the Marine Corps could use Navajo as a code language in voice transmission and that the code would guarantee communications security.

After living among the Navajos for twenty-four years, Johnston was confident that the language he knew would be completely unintelligible to anyone except another Navajo. The language had the additional advantage of being unwritten. In "A Brief History Prepared by the Reference Section History and Museums Division, USMC, May 14, 1982," they explain that Navajo was a rich, fluent language that could be adapted for specialized military terms. For example, the Navajo word for "turtle" represented a tank.

Johnston made his case for the code in a presentation on February 25, 1942. The demonstration included simulated field combat messages composed by the Marines. These messages were given to a Navajo, who then translated it into tribal dialect. The message was transmitted to another Navajo who translated it back to the first in perfect English. The demonstration's success resulted in a recommendation for the recruitment of two hundred Navajos for the program.

The original twenty-nine Navajo Code Talkers, ranging in age from sixteen to eighteen years old, were sent to Camp Eliot near San Diego, put in a room and told to come up with a code in their native language. They developed a code that assigned Navajo words to represent about 450 frequently used military terms that did not exist in the Navajo language.

Reporter Joan Barron covered an entertaining talk to a full house at the National Guard headquarters in Cheyenne (WY) by Samuel Billison, one of the original Code Talkers. Billison said that it was ironic that the same people who punished the Navajos for speaking their own language now wanted them to use that language. Then they were told to tell no one, not even their mothers, about their wartime efforts.

The Navajo language is "very difficult," Billison said, and one word can have fifteen different meanings depending on the tone of voice and emphasis. Billison said that the movie based on the experiences of the Code Talkers in World War II took dramatic license with explaining the difficulty of the language. But he added that he understood why director John Woo made that choice. That explanation would have been "boring."

Consider these examples from the Navajo Code provided by Arlene Hirshfelder and Martha Kreipe in the *Native American Almanac*:

A. Wol-la-chee Ant
B. Shush Bear
C. Mosai Cat

Question 1: The Navajo language was unintelligible to the Japanese because

A. the Navajo language could be adapted to military terms
B. the Navajo language is unwritten
C. the Marine Corps trained the Code Talkers

D. the Japanese did not have access to Navajo speakers
E. Navajo was a rich, fluent language

Commentary

The correct choice is D. This question is difficult unless you are especially alert. You might choose B because the fact that the language is "unwritten" does increase its potential to be used in code. But the word "unintelligible" suggests that the question is looking for an "oral" choice. In the passage, you learn that Navajo is unintelligible to anyone who is not Navajo.

Question 2: You can infer from Samuel Billison's talk

A. that he worked with Philip Johnston
B. that he approved of the John Woo movie
C. that he told his mother about the program
D. that he created the "turtle" name for a tank
E. that he didn't volunteer for the Marine Corps

Commentary

The correct choice is B. The choice is clear if you read only the actual words of Billison. Don't get confused by what is said about the Code Talkers in the rest of the passage. And remember you can usually eliminate a choice like E because it's not positive—or politically correct.

....

The Man Who Saved a President

This passage, adapted from John F. Kennedy's Profiles in Courage, *describes a U.S. Senator who voted against impeachment.*

In a lonely grave lies the man who saved a president, the man who performed what one historian has called "the most heroic act in American history." Yet he is a man whose name few if any of us remember: Edmund G. Ross.

In 1866, when Ross was elected to the U.S. Senate from Kansas, President Andrew Johnson and the Congress were locked in a ferocious battle over how the South should be treated after the Civil War. The president vetoed bill after bill because he thought that Congress wanted to treat the former Confederate states too harshly. Johnson himself was a Southerner. Finally, in complete frustration, the senators decided to get the president out of office. If two-thirds of the senators would vote to impeach Johnson, he would be forced to leave.

Those in the Senate who opposed the president were hopeful that Ross would join their side because he had a long history of opposing slavery. At the age of twenty-eight, Ross had helped rescue a fugitive slave. Later, he had given up his job at a newspaper to enlist in the Union Army.

On March 5, 1868, the impeachment trial began, and before long, observers realized that matters of law were not important to the senators. They wanted Johnson out, and any reason would do.

As the trial neared its conclusion, it became clear that only one more vote was needed to impeach Johnson. The one senator who had not yet announced how he would vote was Edmund Ross. Most people were sure Ross would vote to impeach. "I did not think," said Senator Sumner of Massachusetts, "that a Kansas man could quibble against his country." Yet Ross remained silent, vowing that Johnson should have a fair trial.

As a result of his silence, Ross was pestered, spied upon, and subjected to every kind of pressure, including threats of violence. He was the target of every eye, his name was on every tongue, and his intentions were discussed in every newspaper.

At last the fateful day arrived. Ross described it this way: "The galleries were packed. Tickets of admission were at an enormous premium." Every senator was in his seat, including one who was desperately ill and had to be carried in. When it came time for Ross to vote, the Senate chamber fell silent.

"How say you?" said the Chief Justice. "Is Andrew Johnson guilty or not?"

"I almost literally looked down into my open grave," Ross said later. "Friendships, position, fortune, everything that makes life desirable to an ambitious man were about to be swept away by the breath of my mouth, perhaps forever."

Ross spoke so quietly that he was asked to repeat his answer. And then in a voice that everyone could hear, he said, "Not guilty." The president was saved.

Question 1: Which statement best exemplifies Edmund G. Ross's integrity?

A. He wanted to frustrate the press and fellow senators.
B. He enjoyed the attention that every eye focused on him.
C. Despite loss of friends, position, and fortune, he wanted a fair trial.
D. He wanted Andrew Johnson to remain president.
E. He was against the South.

Commentary

A and B could not be correct because Ross had too much to lose from his decision. E is wrong because Johnson was from the South. D doesn't hold true because nothing shows he was closely associated with Johnson. C is correct. He would stand for "right" at great cost to himself.

Question 2: Which statement best explains why many senators voted for their own desires instead of the good of the country?

A. They opposed slavery.
B. They wanted Johnson out for any reason.
C. They pressured Ross to vote with them.
D. They would no longer be friends with Ross if he didn't vote with them.
E. Matters of law were not important to many senators.

Commentary

A is not valid because while they weren't for slavery, their motive obviously was to punish the South. B is correct as they wanted Johnson out, and the method mattered not to them. C and D are not main points as they would have been satisfied with any other senator's vote, but they just thought Ross might be their best chance. While E is true to some extent, the thrust of their intentions was to eliminate Johnson.

C. Humanities

Mallspeak

This passage is adapted from Peggy Noonan's book What I Saw at the Revolution *and a* Los Angeles Times *article by Elizabeth Mehren. The passage examines the quality of today's oral presentations.*

The irony of modern speeches is that as our ability to disseminate them has exploded (an American president can speak live not only to America but to Europe and to most of the world), the quality has declined.

Why? Lots of reasons, including that we as a nation no longer learn the rhythms of public utterance from Shakespeare and the Bible. When young Lincoln was sprawled in front of the fireplace reading *Julius Caesar*—"Th' abuse of greatness is, when it disjoins remorse from power"—he was, unconsciously, learning to be a poet. You say, "That was Lincoln, not the common man." But the common man was flocking to the docks to get the latest installment of Dickens off the ship from England.

Not so today. Just listen to the insidious proliferation of the youthful sub-dialect known as "mallspeak." Also unlovingly called, in some quarters, "teenbonics." A product of both the urban street scene and the consumer cathedrals of the San Fernando Valley in Los Angeles, mallspeak has made "like" the first word to be a verb, adverb, and conjunction—all at once. "Minimalist," "repetitive," "imprecise," and "inarticulate" are some of the words used to describe mallspeak. Smith College President Ruth Simmons said, "It drives me crazy."

Simmons' concern led to Smith College launching a "speaking across the curriculum" program, featuring "speaking intensive" first-year seminars taught by senior faculty members and an emphasis in many classrooms on oral presentations. At Mount Holyoke, fifteen miles down the road, the speaking, arguing, and writing program started what is believed to be the country's first combined speaking and writing classes.

Mount Holyoke College President Joanne V. Creighton predicts that her school's efforts will be widely emulated. Of course, such changes to the curriculum present new challenges. At Mount Holyoke, biology professor Rachel Fink had qualms about trading some of her students' lab time to accommodate the speaking curriculum. Fink incorporated the curriculum by planning a mock scientific convention, titled, "Out of the Lab and into Your Life," where students distributed research papers and presented extemporaneously their latest findings to their distinguished colleagues. It was a trade-off—because of the time involved, "they didn't get to do fly embryos or chick embryos"—and Fink had her doubts.

But when the day of the convention arrived, Fink was blown away. One team reported on environmental estrogens, hormones that are believed to be reducing fertility levels in many species. The presentation lived up to its catchy title.

"Those students are going to remember 'Impotent Alligators' forever," Fink said.

Still, the mallspeak issue sizzles. Simmons wonders, "Where will we be in another thirty years?"

In retaliation, an editorial in the Smith student newspaper confidently replied: "Like, running the world, you know?"

Question 1: You can infer that biology professor Rachel Fink's major concern with accommodating the speech curriculum was

A. the effectiveness of the "speech across the curriculum" program
B. the students didn't get to do fly or chick embryos
C. where we will be in thirty years

D. teaching the product of the urban street scene
E. trading some of her students' lab time

Commentary

The correct choice is E. Begin by asking yourself what would concern a positive, caring teacher—lost class time for her students. Choice B has some merit, but it's too narrow. The embryos are just an example of Fink's larger concern. The other three choices refer to other people's concerns or to other programs.

Question 2: You can infer that the "public utterance" in line 6

A. is the insidious proliferation of a youthful sub-dialect
B. suffers from the teaching of Shakespeare
C. has declined because of "teenbonics"
D. benefits from the reading of Dickens
E. disjoins remorse from power

Commentary

The correct choice is D. Again, you need to focus on the specific context of the phrase "public utterance" and ignore the rest of the passage. Even if you hadn't read the passage, you would probably choose D because it is the most positive response.

....

The Dull Knifes of Pine Ridge by Joe Starita

This book examines four generations in the life of a Lakota Sioux family—from the Battle at Little Bighorn to Desert Storm.

Walking point was among the most hazardous assignments of the Vietnam War. On jungle patrol, search-and-destroy missions and routine reconnaissance, the point man walked ahead of the main soldier body. The trails were laced with trip wires, covered with booby traps and land mines, and contained the camouflaged "pungi pits," deep holes filled with sharpened bamboo stakes embedded upright on the bottom, stakes that were often coated with the urine of water buffalo to induce infection. Dense foliage on either side of the trail offered numerous ambush possibilities, and it was often the eyes and ears of the point man, and an innate sense of danger, that determined whether those who followed arrived home in a black, zippered body bag, a wheelchair or walking on their own.

"They thought because I was Indian," explained Guy Dull Knife, "I could see the bushes and the trees moving in the jungle better than the white soldiers and the black soldiers, so they made me walk point right from the beginning. And for all I know, they may have been right. During the whole time I walked point for my company, we only lost eighteen men."

That first night, and every night for the next few weeks, Guy Dull Knife was taught how to walk point by a middle-aged Vietnamese man. The former Communist had fought the French in the '50s and the Americans throughout much of the '60s. After the North Vietnamese Army had wiped out a South Vietnamese village, killing a number of his relatives, he had flipped sides and volunteered to work for the U.S. military. The army had assigned him to the 196th Light Infantry and he became what was known as a "Kit Carson scout" during the Vietnam War.

"He spoke pretty decent English, and as we were getting ready to go out that first night, he asked me what my name was. I told him and he looked kind of puzzled, so I said I was an American Indian. He looked at me for a while and then he started to smile. He put his hand to his mouth and made a few war whoops. 'Like in a John Wayne movie, huh?' I laughed and said, 'Yeah, just like in a John Wayne movie.'"

During their weeks together, the middle-aged man taught the young soldier how to read the jungle floor for booby traps and showed him the best places to camp. His nickname was Papa-san, and in broken English, he explained the military tactics of the NVA [North Vietnamese Army], how they fought and how they thought, their battle habits, strategy and techniques. And he told Guy when and why an ambush was most likely.

"He was small and wiry and tough and I remember he could walk forever without complaining. He always carried a rucksack with him, stocked with the kind of foods he liked. Every once in a while, he would throw a couple of chickens in the sack before we started out. If he thought it was safe, he'd pull out a chicken and kill it."

Sometimes, the Lakota Indian from Pine Ridge and the Kit Carson scout from Vietnam would squat on their haunches, roasting fresh chicken together in a small clearing in the Asian jungle.

"I got along with the Vietnamese real well the whole time I was there. We kind of looked alike in some ways and it seemed to make a difference. To me and them."

Question 1: Guy Dull Knife's attitude toward the Vietnamese could best be described as:

A. patronizing
B. indulgent
C. empathetic
D. superior
E. admiring

Commentary

We learn in the passage that Guy Dull Knife strikes up a friendship with his Vietnamese mentor, a former Communist who fought against the Americans before changing sides. He discovers that they can share food together and even look alike to some degree. This all causes Guy to feel empathetic, choice C, toward the Vietnamese. A (patronizing) and D (superior) are both wrong because they suggest that Guy felt the Vietnamese were his inferiors. B might be true of the Vietnamese trainer who helped Guy learn how to walk point, but it's not true of Guy himself. E (admiring) is not the case—the guide was, after all, a former enemy of the United States, but it's not too far from the truth.

Question 2: Why does the author tell us that the Vietnamese trainer was a former Communist and an enemy of the United States?

A. As an Indian, Guy Dull Knife's ancestors were former enemies of the U.S. government.
B. It highlights the difficulty American soldiers had in telling friendly and unfriendly Vietnamese apart.
C. By telling us the trainer's bad traits first, the author deepens the character's development—we see both good and bad sides.
D. He wants us to dislike the trainer.
E. The author wants to show how Guy might prejudge the trainer.

Commentary

A is true but doesn't contribute to the development of the passage. B is also true, but again, it is not relevant to the significant events the narrator relates. C is the best answer because the author uses this technique to create a multidimensional character. D is false—the narrator clearly wants us to see why Guy came to like the trainer, and while E might be the case, the trainer's crack about John Wayne would be more likely to offend Guy.

D. Fiction

"Shadowboxing" by Bill Kloefkorn

This excerpt from the short story "Shadowboxing" concerns a teenager and a skinny-dipping episode.

From Shannon's sand pit to Doc Montzingo's office on Main Street is a distance of three miles; as the crow flies, the distance is reduced to slightly more than two miles. But distance can be less a matter of miles than of attitude, of discretion, of unmitigated guts, as Galen Grigsby learned that warm afternoon in early July when he went skinny-dipping with the newest girl in town, Julie Beresford.

Julie had moved to Danville with her mother and father in late December, between semesters, and Galen first saw her, or became seriously aware of her, when she took her seat in front of him in Miss Stevens's literature class. She was thin and dark-eyed and not very tall—Galen guessed that the top of her head might reach the underside of his chin—with hair long and immeasurably thick and black.

She was striking without being exactly pretty, her nose perhaps too long, her smile perhaps too crooked. And the contrast between the darkness of her hair and the fairness of her skin was maybe too distinct, as if she were a photograph unduly frontlighted by the sun.

But Galen had been taken with her from the beginning, though several months would have to pass before he'd admit it, and even then the words would not come easily. In the meantime he sat behind her in Miss Stevens's class, studying her hair. He tried to imagine its thickness being thinned by water, by rainwater, say, thickness ebony and wet, its sheen emerging slowly as the hair dried.

He didn't want to touch the hair as much as he wanted to admire it, to see and appreciate it as not only an extension of a vital and breathing body, but also as a focal point on a work of art, the feature that the artist had singled out to enhance so precisely, so splendidly, that the beholder's eye would sooner or later be unable to ignore it.

Galen studied the hair each morning during first period, inhaled it, memorized it, though his fascination with blackness and sheen did not prevent him from hearing what Miss Stevens had to say. She was a young, perky woman who wore thick glasses and smiled easily, and Galen admired her because she often looked at him but rarely asked him questions.

She seemed to understand his shyness and to respect it. She seemed also to respect his intelligence: He knew the answers, and therefore to call on him would only underscore an aptitude that embarrassed Galen more often than it pleased him.

Question 1: Galen Grigsby's mind could handle imaginary and real situations at the same time quite easily as shown by one of the following:

A. He could imagine regular distance or distance as the crow flies at the same time he was swimming.
B. He thought of Julie as if she were a photograph even as he contrasted the darkness of her hair and fairness of her skin.
C. He was mentally memorizing Julie's hair even as he took in everything his teacher said.
D. He could look and analyze Julie's hair as he imagined it as a point of art.
E. Galen knew the answers in class but preferred not to be called on.

Commentary

C shows him clearly imagining, but at the same time filling his mind with lessons, which are definitely two separate workings of the mind. In A he could use his mind to imagine and swim automatically. B seems to be two sides of imagining as is true of D. E shows only that he could think but didn't want to tell his thinking.

Question 2: With which of the following statements would the author most likely agree?

A. It's a long, long way from Doc Montzingo's office to the sand pit.
B. Julie's beauty was immediately apparent to everyone.
C. Galen is obsessed with people's hair.
D. Galen's shyness disguises his intelligence.
E. Miss Stevens doesn't call on Galen because he wouldn't know the answer.

Commentary

The distance between the office and the sand pit in A is two or three miles, but it's the psychic distance that the narrator is concerned with. At this point we can't be sure whether that's large or small. In B Julie is pretty, but not too pretty, and only Galen feels attracted to her. C is too narrow—we know that Galen is fascinated with Julie's hair, but not with other people's. D represents the best answer because Miss Stevens realizes that Galen doesn't want people to know just how smart he is. E is wrong because it states the opposite of the truth—Miss Stevens doesn't call on Galen because he *would* know the answer.

....

Brush with the Real World

This story was written by a college student, Lisa German, looking back on her high school graduation.

A few months before graduation from high school, one of 1
my good friends, Katy, and I decided that we wanted to take a road trip after we graduated. We decided that camping for

four days would be perfect. We tried to recruit several of our friends to join us in this excursion, but all had prior engagements or could not get permission from their parents.

With graduation right around the corner, Katy and I carefully started making arrangements. We made list after list of items that we needed from the grocery store, and packing lists to ensure that we would have everything for the journey. As the excitement from commencement began to diminish, the excitement for the trip mounted; Katy and I looked forward to our own commencement in the real world.

My parents were wary of two girls, only eighteen, spending three nights in the wilderness by themselves, exposed to all that hinders mankind. My dad was also concerned about the weather, as it was only the latter half of May; what if we became trapped in the hills with not enough clothing to keep us warm from a snowstorm? What if there were some crazed lunatic wandering in the forest, waiting to prey on innocent and unsuspecting teenaged girls? His constant questions put a little fear in my mind. But I was more determined to take my chance at a few days of freedom and to use the opportunity to show my parents that we could make it out there on our own.

As the day of departure drew near, I became a little more nervous about the trip. What if my dad were right? This could be it for me—my last chance. I forced these thoughts aside. On the morning before we left, I wrote a note to my parents: "Mom and Dad, don't worry about me. Everything is going to be okay. See you on Sunday, probably late. I love you."

We were off, just Katy and me and the world which lay ahead of us.

. . .

Once we reached our campsite, the sun had begun to sink into the clouds. The crosswind coming off the lake threatened to put out the fire we were trying so desperately to keep lit. We gathered branches from nearby, constructing a makeshift shelterbelt to block the gusts. As we were putting the finishing touches on the "wall," we heard a loud vehicle, not too far away. Katy and I nervously looked at one another, realizing just how vulnerable we were. By that time, there was no one left fishing on the lake; we were alone, or so we thought.

A dirty white pickup crawled around the bend, coming into view. Two scraggly men hung out of the windows. I yanked my hat off the table and put it on. Katy ran into the tent, leaving only her backside visible. Our intentions were for them to think that we were men. They pulled around the curve, ever so slowly, gawking all the while. I held my breath. My chest was tight, not knowing what to expect. A sigh of relief came over me as the truck pulled past without any exchange of words. Just when I thought it was all over, the pickup backed up. It stopped right in front of our campsite for a couple of seconds, they gave a little wave, and then continued on their way.

Katy and I caught each other's eyes. She ran over to me, wondering what we were supposed to do. We did the only thing that seemed logical at the time; we pulled out the video camera. We began to describe what had just happened. "Check our cameras," we instructed. We had plans to take a picture so that if anything happened to us, at least the men would be identifiable and could be caught.

The low growl emanating from the truck could be heard for nearly an hour after the incident. Katy and I tried to distract ourselves by making dinner and talking about guys we liked. We wandered to the lakeshore. As night drew on, we sat by the fire, still leery about the events that had taken place.

Before climbing into the tent, we made sure no one was lurking around. Just as we turned the lantern out, we started to hear it again. Gravel rumbled under the tires. We began to think we might be killed. As the truck seemed to close the distance between us, Katy and I had had enough. I grabbed the hatchet and the pocketknife, she grabbed the pepper spray and car keys, and we dashed for the car.

Katy put the keys in the ignition and locked the doors, ready to drive away at any moment. We lowered the window slightly so that we could hear all that was going on outside the safety of the car. My heart was racing. We had tears in our eyes.

After what seemed like an eternity, the sound of the pickup became more distant. We looked at one another and started laughing. Nervous laughter. We cautiously opened the doors. Walking out into the open, we looked up. The stars were like nothing I had ever seen before. Breathtaking. I could finally breathe normally again.

It was then that I realized that maybe my parents' fears were legitimate. I saw that I would not always be under their protection. The real world can be a scary place, but at the same time, absolutely amazing.

Question 1: Repeated warnings from the narrator's parents only make her more determined to go on the trip. Which of the following was not a legitimate reason for concern?

A. Some of their friends could not get permission from their parents to go on the camping trip.
B. The narrator's father was worried about unpredictable weather.
C. The girls were only eighteen.
D. Dangerous people are fairly common in wilderness areas.
E. The girls could become lost in the hills.

Commentary

Notice the key word "not." It's easy to skip over that and not realize what the question is really asking. All answers are mentioned in the passage except D which is brought up strictly as a hypothetical situation—a "what if?", in other words.

Question 2: Which is the best definition for "emanating" as used in line 64?

A. withdraw
B. come forth
C. arise
D. exhale
E. radiate

Commentary

The best answer is B, "come forth." A, "withdraw," means just the opposite of *emanate*. Answer C, "arise," suggests coming out of sleep or dormancy; D suggests breathing; and E, "radiate," means to spread in a large circle.

Paired Passages

These passages are adapted from the Lincoln-Douglas Debate cases of Stephen Davis and Ben Silberman (Des Moines Roosevelt H.S., Iowa—coached by David Huston). The students are debating whether equality is better than liberty in achieving a just social order. Passage 1 supports an egalitarian society. Passage 2 supports a society based on personal responsibility.

Passage 1

All just social orders attempt to respect their citizens. An egalitarian society works toward this goal by beginning with the assumption that every individual has the same moral worth. An egalitarian society works to ensure that everyone has the tools he needs to succeed and the equal consideration needed to use these tools.

Libertarian systems take a radically different approach. They attempt to respect people by creating a laissez-faire social order, a system where there are as few restrictions as possible. While this can be an effective economic plan, as a social policy it is disastrous. In *The Hungry Spirit*, Charles Handy explains: "The drive for efficiency may erode the very civilization that it is designed to promote, because its benefits do not fall equally, nor do its costs . . . 20 percent of the people . . . seem to get 80 percent of the wealth."

While differences in wealth aren't inherently bad, in a libertarian society money is more than just a means to get goods. Money and respect become one and the same because money buys opportunities. As a result, the child who grows up in an inner-city ghetto and attends a substandard school never gets the basic tools she needs to succeed.

What is truly unjust is that the child did nothing to deserve this fate. Her parents' economic status should not have kept her from the opportunities she was due as a human being.

Life is equally unjust for those fortunate enough to benefit. Why? Because no matter how hard a person works, the achievements mean little if many people didn't even get the chance to compete. In short, winning a social race is essentially meaningless if an entire class never makes it to the starting line.

Passage 2

In order to maintain any just social order, some basic services must exist. No government, libertarian, egalitarian, or any other, could survive without providing basic services like education and law enforcement.

But basic services are not enough. We must have personal responsibility as individuals. Freedom and responsibility are as inseparable as two sides of the same coin. When you claim the freedom to take an action, you must also accept the responsibility for the consequences of that action. For example, the freedom to have a child comes with the responsibility to take care of that child. While having a duty may sound undesirable, responsibility is not the price of freedom, it is the reward. Responsibility is what keeps our lives from being trivial.

The government cannot take on all responsibility for us. Nor is government always necessary to regulate society. When a person is poor, we provide that person with welfare; when a person is too wealthy, we levy a progressive tax; when a person is excluded from a private club, the government intervenes. This intervention is well-intentioned but destructive to the social order because it displaces working societal checks.

In his book *What It Means to Be a Libertarian*, Charles Murray gives an example of what happened when the government tried to take on the personal responsibility of family planning: "Parental pressures and social stigma . . . kept illegitimacy rare, and private charitable adoption services coped with the residual problem. . . . Informal, but effective, this civil system could not withstand the proliferation of welfare benefits for single mothers."

When individual responsibility was taken over by the government, the problem got worse. People further shed their personal responsibilities because they thought the government would take up the slack. A permanent welfare class was created and many more people suffered. Quite simply, government-built social institutions fail.

Question 1: In Passage 1, which one of the following best captures the meaning of the word "egalitarian" in line 2?

A. laissez-faire
B. moral worth
C. libertarian
D. social order
E. opportunities

Commentary

The correct choice is E. Although the passage is discussing "moral worth," you can tell from the context that the author wants a society built on equality. And equality means more opportunities for everyone.

Question 2: In Passage 2, freedom and responsibility are inseparable because

A. an unnecessary duty is undesirable
B. responsibility is the reward of freedom
C. that's the price of a progressive tax

D. government is necessary to regulate society
E. the government can't care for children

Commentary

The correct choice is B. Again, study the specific context rather than the surrounding arguments. You might be tempted to choose E, but that's an example and not the basic principle discussed.

In the immortal words of Zippy the Pinhead, "Are we having fun yet?"

About the Authors

Randall McCutcheon, nationally recognized by the U.S. Department of Education for innovation in curriculum, has authored eight books, including *Can You Find It?*, a guide to teaching research skills to high school students, which received the 1990 Ben Franklin Award for best self-help book of the year; *Get Off My Brain*, a survival guide for students who hate to study, which was selected by the New York Public Library as one of 1998's Best Books for Teenagers; and three textbooks for speech and journalism courses.

After nearly a decade working in radio and television, McCutcheon taught for twenty-seven years in both public and private schools in Iowa, Massachusetts, Nebraska, and New Mexico. He was selected the State Teacher of the Year in Nebraska in 1985, and in 1987 he was named the National Forensic League National Coach of the Year. Elected to the N.F.L. Hall of Fame in 2001, he concluded a successful career as a high school speech coach. In twenty-seven years, his speech teams won twenty-five state and five national championships.

James Schaffer is the chair of the English Department at Nebraska Wesleyan University where he teaches writing and journalism courses. He has a Ph.D. in English from the University of Virginia and has been frequently involved in developing writing curricula, assisting with a freshman writing program, and leading writing workshops. He is the author of three textbooks and numerous articles.

Schaffer was a finalist for the Teacher-in-Space program in 1985 and, as a result, became a speaker and presenter for NASA. He has given more than four hundred programs on the space shuttle to professional organizations, community groups, and schools. He was named Nebraska's Aerospace Educator of the Year.

As a journalism advisor, he has lead his publication's staffs to numerous state and national awards, including the Best Magazine of the Year award from the Columbia Scholastic Press Association. Schaffer and his wife, Mary Lynn, also an educator, have three children—Suzanne, Sarah, and Stephen—two dogs, and a cat.